somewhere

a place, a cause, a legacy

"A wonderfully personal story of finding oneself in a new world - charmed by its inhabitants while appalled at lack of access to basic things like education. Judith Pasco's telling of how she has supported young women is refreshingly clear and honest. She does not shrink from including the inevitable failures and shows that even these are at least a partial success."

Walter (Chip) Morris, Jr., author of <u>Living Maya</u>

"Judith Pasco offers an inspirational invitation to 'find your passion and apply it to a cause you love.' Her travels to Central America and beyond broke open her heart and her worldview and as a result we see the possibility of one person making a difference. 'One of my favorite prayers,' she writes, 'is that I be open to opportunity and that I allow myself to be drawn to possibilities.' May it be so for each of us."

Jack Nelson-Pallmeyer, associate professor of Justice and Peace Studies at the University of St. Thomas and author of <u>Authentic Hope: It's the End of the World but Soft Landings are Possible</u>

"Judith shows each of us how using the power of our minds, our voices, and our compassionate hearts can bring positive change to humanity's suffering."

Surinder Moore, Program Director, Alternative Gifts International

"What is striking in Mrs. Pasco's book is the deep empathy she has for these disadvantaged young women. Over the years, she has taken the time during her travels and experiences in this region to study not only the Mayan culture, but also the female culture of the indigenous woman. She has evidenced deep-seated racism and gender discrimination which profoundly impedes educational opportunities for Mayan women. However, her determination, tenacity, and sensitivity are qualities that have served her well in her quest to use education to liberate them."

Frances Dixon, Founder and President, Adopt-a -Village in Guatemala

somewhere for my soul to go

a place, a cause, a legacy

Judith Pasco

Produced by:

FriesenPress
Suite 300 – 852 Fort Street
Victoria, BC, Canada V8W 1H8

www.friesenpress.com

Distributed to the trade by The Ingram Book Company

Why not go out on a limb? That's where the fruit is.

.

Will Rogers

Dedicated to:

Eric, my other legacy, my son, my friend

Bob, who insisted we go to Guatemala in 1990

Linda, my only friend (according to her), for her endless badgering that I write the story of Mujeres de Maiz Opportunity Foundation

TABLE OF CONTENTS

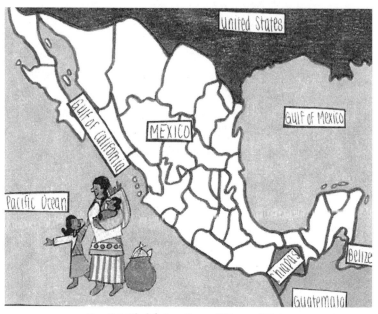

San Cristóbal de Las Casas, Chiapas, México

Maps by Jenna Hall (used with permission)

PROLOGUE

I'm a listmaker. I'm telling you this because there are lists included in this book. I have found that lists can simplify, clarify and take the place of expiring brain cells. The older I become, the more I rely on lists. I include a few here for your perusal.

1. Things I need to do
2. Things I am grateful for*
3. Things I need to take on trips
4. Good things that happened today
5. Countries I have visited
6. Countries I want to visit
7. My most fascinating experiences
8. My best decisions
9. My worst decisions
10. Cats I have had
11. Meals I'll fix for houseguests.

From the above you might start to get an idea of me and my anal, a bit compulsive, personality. Here's a second list about what cannot be deduced from the first list.

A mental list before going to sleep

List of information about me NOT implied in the first list

1. Majored in Spanish at Indiana University

2. Managed a dental office for 12 years

3. Taught Spanish at the high school level for 20 years

4. Have a son, Eric

5. Lived in Denmark for a year (1988-89) on the tiny island of Bornholm in the Baltic Sea ... a story not included in the upcoming pages

6. Been with my current husband for 22 years

7. Board chair and founder of *Mujeres de Maiz OF*

8. LOVE Latin American folk art

9. Have a weakness for dark chocolate

Facts, all facts, and admittedly, a bit dry. What follows is a journey: a journey of aging, introspection, growth and learning curves; a journey with friends and supporters that has culminated in my legacy; a journey showing why it's not too late to begin something new and good and why we should espouse at least one cause. Damn, I think I just wrote another list.

Judith Pasco

INTRODUCTION

Travelers are risk takers. Risk taking ranges from "minimum" (those who may travel but don't want to experience much outside what is familiar and within their comfort zone) to the other extreme of "maximum" (which includes mountain climbers, those who practice extreme sports, those that knowingly go into areas of war or corridors of crime, etc.)

My father, Hubert Jagger, was a risk taker. Born in 1899 in Yorkshire, England, he enlisted in the British Army in 1917 at the age of 17 and served in WWI in Russia, Turkey and Saudi Arabia. When the war ended, he found himself back in his small village. Many of the young men had been killed, and many of the survivors had been terribly damaged by mustard gas. For a year my father passed most of his time in the local pub and was perceived as a lost cause. But then he had an offer from a cousin in New Jersey: His passage (in steerage) to the States would be paid if he'd work for a year in a machine shop. At the end of his rope, defeated by war and basically aimless, my father accepted.

After a year in New Jersey and ready for something new, Hubert traveled to Texas where he made his living by boxing. He had been a featherweight boxer in the army and was quick on his feet. In between fights, he washed dishes and visualized possible paths his life might take.

My father wasn't one to let his brain atrophy. He and his older brother had been the first two boys from his village to escape the coal mine and graduate from Whitney Mount Grammar School (the equivalent of our high school.) So he moved again, this time north to Chicago, and by working diligently he graduated from college with a degree in mechanical engineering.

At the age of 27 he married my mother, Eunice, then 18, and settled down to a life of work. His risk taking diminished over the years. Seeing himself secure financially, finally, after raising my three siblings during the Depression, he moved to the other end of the risk-taking scale. He began to avoid risks. His fear of losing what he had worked so hard to accomplish overrode the risks of youth ... fighting wars, moving to another continent, leaving family, etc. Hubert continued to love to travel but the trips my mother and he took were not adventurous. They took tours in Europe, visited the family in England, vacationed in the Caribbean. Their most adventurous trips were on freighters that went around the world, stopping at ports in the Middle and Far East.

When I was born, my father was almost 50, my mother, 39. My siblings were 20, 17 and 15. My recollection of my father is of a gray, then white haired, balding man who was already in his late 60s when I graduated from high school. I have always regretted coming along so late in their lives, as my parents died — a mere two weeks apart — in 1987, when I was just 39.

I come by my travel addiction honestly. I also think that I am farther along the "risk taker" scale than was my father. I have enjoyed traveling alone. Not knowing the language of where I travel is not a deterrent. I have traveled in unsettled regions: El Salvador right before the peace accords were signed; Nicaragua, just after Daniel Ortega lost the presidency to Violeta Chamarro; Chiapas, Mexico, during the elections of

1997, observing burning ballot boxes and blocked roads. But any risks I take are considered, and are neither extreme nor life-threatening. I want to experience countries and cultures from the ground, not from a tour bus.

Four years ago, my husband and I joined a friend of ours from India in a monthlong adventure that included a road trip from Ahmedabad to Delhi as well as visits to Khajuraho and Varanasi. In the airport in Varanasi we were talking with people from Iowa, who had been on a tour that also included Delhi, Agra and Jaipur. A woman about my age commented on how wonderful the tour was.

"When we were in Delhi," she marveled, "we stayed in a lovely hotel. Anything we wanted, our guide went out and got for us. We didn't have to go out in the streets at all!" She added what a bargain the tour was, costing only $4,300 per person from Iowa for 12 days. Her comments saddened me in ways I'm not sure she would have understood. Walking around the alleys of Delhi was exhilarating. Eating at local establishments, including the "truck stops" when we were on the road, was experiencing India more as a traveler than a tourist. And the cost for our 30-day trip was far less, including purchases.

My parents died within two weeks of each other in 1987 after a 60-year marriage. With my share of the inheritance money, I moved myself and my then 15-year-old son to Bornholm, a Danish island in the Baltic, for a year of change and new experiences. There is nothing, absolutely nothing (and this is something I have uttered repeatedly to my students) like living in another country to broaden one's perspective. World news is presented differently and points of view are obviously not centered on the United States.

Son Eric and I made good traveling companions. We took advantage of cheap flights from Copenhagen and visited Spain, Italy, England, Turkey and Tunisia. We shared amazing adventures that proved invaluable in strengthening a mother-son bond that endures today. Thinking back on this time together, two "adventures" come readily to mind.

Antalya, Turkey, on the Mediterranean coast is a lovely city. Having flown from Copenhagen on a Spies (pronounced "Speese") tour, we were staying in a small, family-run guesthouse. The package included flight and hotel and the rest was up to us. It was a running joke in Denmark that the Danes were so inept at international espionage that they wrote "Spies" on the outside of the buses.

A dolmus is a van that serves as a taxi, and Eric and I caught the one that was heading to the Düden Şelalesi Waterfall Park. The park didn't disappoint. It was refreshing to walk among the waterfalls and pools on a hot day. The family picnics amazed us as the women brought small stoves and were doing normal everyday cooking at the park while the men lounged, talked and smoked.

We hadn't brought food because we had been told of a restaurant along the river bank just outside the park boundaries. But to get there we had to leave from the main entrance, rejoin the road and circle around to where we thought the restaurant would be. We made our way to the river and found it running noisily along. But no restaurant. We turned again, so we were heading back in the direction of the waterfall park, and came to a couple of picnic tables. Nothing else gave us an indication of a restaurant, so we sat down to come up with the next plan. Almost immediately, out of nowhere, a man appeared at our table. "Fish?" he asked. "Fish," we answered, and he was gone.

After about 20 minutes, he reappeared with soft drinks and covered clay casserole dishes hiding the baked fresh fish. It was delicious. We still couldn't figure out where the man had come from.

After the meal, we spotted an interesting path that looked as if it would lead to a better view of the backside of the waterfall park. The path climbed up a hill and ran along the side of the embankment. We could see a cave just up ahead on the left and as we approached, a huge bulldog leapt out barking and growling. I almost had a heart attack before I realized that he was chained inside the cave and his chain didn't quite reach the path. But it was close enough to make us both think of the Indiana Jones movies with the scary traps set for unsuspecting explorers. We got our view, but the adrenalin rush stayed with us all the way back to our guesthouse.

Another inexpensive Spies charter flight took us to Tunisia. After sightseeing in Tunis, exploring Carthage and walking around Sousse with its amazing souk, we booked a three-day bus trip that took us south, past the troglodyte dwellings used in the first Star Wars movie, and out to the edge of the Sahara desert. Just before dawn the next morning, we were on camels heading for the sand. The air was still and warm, and it was a joy to share this with Eric. I could see that something like this was beyond any expectations he could have had. We didn't have to venture far into the desert to get an idea of its vastness, its coloring, its softness and, at the same time, its inherently forbidding aspect.

Within six weeks of our returning to the Seattle area, I met Bob. He had always had a desire to visit Maya territory and his interest sparked my own. A year later, we were taking off to Guatemala for a month. It was a life-changing trip.

I fell in love with Guatemala. The bright colors, the food, the dramatic scenery, the distinctive huipiles (women's blouses hand woven on backstrap looms). I was hooked. And yet there was a lot I didn't understand. I knew almost nothing of the civil war, the disappearances and displaced persons in the hundreds of thousands and the impunity of the military.

I came away enthralled and curious and spent a year devouring everything I could get my hands on about the politics, economics, culture, spirituality and history of Central America. I learned that the United States, my own country, had meddled, interfered and had done what was necessary ... at times no matter the human cost ... to shore up our economic interests.

Central America attracted me like a magnet. I traveled five times to different parts of Guatemala, made more than a dozen visits to Chiapas in Southern Mexico, and once participated in a delegation to El Salvador and Nicaragua. I was not yet aware that these trips and experiences were forming a basis, a mindset, for what eventually would turn into a non-profit foundation. Although at this point I had no future plan, I found myself raising money for women that had been severely impacted by the civil wars. I continued to read voraciously. In 2000, a friend and I marched at Fort Benning, Georgia, in protest against the infamous School of the Americas, which had trained numerous Latin American military leaders in torture techniques and low intensity warfare. Among many documented incidents, one that stands out for me is the assassination of Archbishop Romero of El Salvador by soldiers trained at the Fort Benning facility. The popular Romero had been advocating for rights for the poor, which threatened the existing financial/military/political power base.

The thousands of protestors consisted of a high percentage of nuns, priests and ministers. Most of us crossed the line demarcating the boundary of the army base. We understood that we could leave at any time by boarding military buses that would carry us off the base. Instead, the buses took us to a processing center where we were arrested and fingerprinted. I received a five-year Ban and Bar notice, indicating that if I were to trespass again on an army base, I would be prosecuted.

I felt more and more that Central America had received a raw deal ever since the conquest. Chiapas (although Mexico is officially designated as North America) falls into this category as it used to belong to Guatemala. Somehow I wanted to help.

I wrote a guest editorial for the Peninsula Daily News of Port Angeles in 2010 that explained how important I think it is to find a cause.

POINT OF VIEW

A week or so ago I saw a photo in the Peninsula Daily News of three women in Port Townsend dressed as teacups. They had made a commitment to raise funds for an organization that builds schools in Pakistan and Afghanistan.

About eighteen years ago, I was raising money for an indigenous group in Guatemala. An old friend of mine, learning of my efforts, said to me, "One person can't make a difference. Problems are just too severe. My philosophy is to live my life the best I can and consciously tune out these hopeless causes that I don't even want to know about."

Her statement stopped me in my tracks. I knew in my heart that not only was she wrong, but she was also depriving herself of incredible gifts by not finding a cause.

Find a cause. Find a cause that resonates with you. Find a cause that speaks to your passion….whether it be education, music, food, justice, reading, animals, a local service organization, or an international program. If your personal interest isn't mirrored in an existing program, start one of your own.

Dedication to a cause can take many forms that may include a donation of money, a commitment of time or effort, solidarity, or just running errands or stuffing envelopes.

I speak from experience. The locally based *Mujeres de Maiz Opportunity Foundation* of which I am Board Chair, has in five short years greatly impacted a cooperative of indigenous women in Chiapas, Mexico. By providing them with resources for education that include scholarships, literacy training, children's programs, workshops, eye glasses, etc, we have given women and girls a voice and a choice in their destiny. We board members work hard, true, but it is the most rewarding work there is.

Living here on the Olympic Peninsula, we are a bit isolated. Becoming involved in a local cause will connect you at a deeper level with our community and the people in it. For the many senior citizens who live here, volunteering is a way to keep active and create meaningful social contacts. As we age, being part of a larger group keeps us mentally stimulated.

Linking up with a national or international group will propel you into the global community and enable you to establish dialogues with like-minded individuals the world over. It provides a perspective and understanding otherwise difficult to attain. A friend of mine spent two years in the Peace Corps in Macedonia after she retired. Another retiree is currently volunteering in an elementary school in Spain for two months. If physical travel is a problem, the internet provides us with virtual travel and worldwide connections.

I am hopeful and impressed by the numbers of young people who plan to dedicate their lives to meaningful causes. When talking to high school seniors about to graduate, a good number are pursuing paths that will allow them to make a difference in the world.

I truly believe that if each of us dedicates some part of our life to others, we will all ultimately benefit. One person can indeed make a difference, and people striving together can have an even bigger impact. So hats off to those women in teacup costumes, to those senior citizens who selflessly serve others, and to those teens who already are thinking of the less fortunate.

Find a cause. You'll be amazed at what you reap.

I wrote this book to elaborate on how I found my cause. Or perhaps my cause found me. I hope you find yours.

June, 2012

Note: The names of the women and others with whom I work in Chiapas have been changed to protect their privacy.

PART I

LAYING A FOUNDATION

BELIZE AND GUATEMALA

Martha, Carol and I are sitting on kitchen chairs that would match nicely with a formica table from the '50s. The chairs are somehow fastened to a large canoe and we are peacefully motoring up the San Pedro River from Naranjo, Guatemala, to Mexico. Martha is a bit sunburned. We are relaxed and it's not too humid. The past 10 days have been incredibly humid and I've been aware that my normally excited travel attitude has been eroding in this sticky, steamy sauna heat. The hours on the river with the refreshing breeze allow me some reflection time in what has proved to be a very adventurous trip thus far.

Martha and I met in 1971, in a "previous life" when we were young and in first marriages, raising kids and working. Through divorces and job changes and my move from Southern California to the Pacific Northwest, we had stayed in touch. But in the early 1990s, our friendship was cemented when she came to visit me in Seattle and we had a "Thelma and Louise" weekend. We danced the night away at a real dive and we were the classiest "broads" that place had seen in a long time. We'll never forget an exchange we had across the table that night. The band was loud and we had to yell to be heard. Martha had just returned to the table after a dance. The conversation went like this:

"... joint."

"What?" I yelled back. "This place is a joint?"

"... joint!!!"

"What??? He wanted you to have a joint???"

"No," Martha was practically screaming, "He just got out of the joint!!!"

We looked at each, enthralled and horrified. We were definitely out of our everyday environment.

At Pike Place Market the following day, we browsed through handbags pretending to look for ones big enough to house our imaginary guns. Through silliness and laughing, we bonded.

Martha's only travel had been to Hawaii. In June 1995, I told her that Carol and I were planning a three-week trip through Belize, Guatemala and Mexico, and she expressed some interest. About four weeks before the departure date, she called me and opened the conversation with, "I know I've had a couple glasses of wine, but I want to go with you."

"But Marth," I enjoined, "We have our tickets already and we leave in a month."

"I can do it," she answered.

"But Marth, you need a passport."

"I can do it."

And she did. And she loved it. And she's told me many times that that trip opened up her world.

Carol was a fellow teacher at Decatur High School in Federal Way, just south of Seattle. We were hired at the same time and were colleagues for five years before I moved to take a position on the Olympic Peninsula. She and I had traveled together a couple of times and we found that we made good travel partners. (Since this trip, Carol and I have made at least ten more journeys together.) I admired her tremendously because she had to overcome certain fears to travel: the fear of not being in very close touch with loved ones, the fear of catching some strange disease, and the fear that something would happen to me and she'd have to manage on her own. I didn't have those fears or I didn't have the sense to have those fears. I admired her bravery.

Ten days before our trip down the San Pedro River, we landed in Belize City: three middle-aged women and my son, Eric, who had just celebrated his 22nd birthday. Eric is an ideal travel companion. He is an adventurous eater; he welcomes new experiences; he is a people person and he doesn't complain. I hadn't traveled with him since we had lived in Denmark six years earlier and I was looking forward to his company and intrepid sense of humor.

In search of an adventure and after much research, I had figured out an itinerary that included a mixture of culture, action and a bit of uncertainty. Getting off the plane in Belize was like running full speed into a wall of heat. I could almost squeeze the moisture out of the air with my hand. It was like breathing underwater. After one night under mosquito-netted beds in what some consider a dangerous city, we took buses to Cave Branch retreat, a jungle camp in the middle of nowhere. If you look up Cave Branch today, you'll find a much more sophisticated adventure camp, but in 1995 it was definitely on the rudimentary side. Showers and hair washings took place in the river.

The following morning we met Jacinto, our Cave Branch guide, who had lived his whole life in this part of Belize. He and his machete led us into the jungle. He showed us survival skills that included how to catch fish using a deadly vine, where to find drinkable water, what plants to avoid. We were enthralled. We saw giant anthills and jaguar claw marks 6 feet up on the bark of a tree. Jacinto told us of natural remedies and how when his brother had been bitten by the deadly poisonous fer-de-lance snake, he had been able to save his life by knowing which leaves and herbs were antidotal.

The following day found us riding a tractor and carrying giant inner-tubes. Jacinto took us through endless grapefruit orchards and finally stopped by a path that led to the river. Although I managed to get myself gracelessly into the inner tube, I immediately found the current too strong for me. I looked at Carol and Martha and saw that they were struggling as well. Extricating myself from the tube should probably have been filmed for "Clumsiest Videos." As an alternative route we walked with our tubes along the edge of the river in the jungle until the river disappeared into a cave opening that yawned huge. Inside the cave, the paddling was easier. Once we had turned the corner, our headlamps, connected to batteries around our necks, were essential. We "parked" the inner tubes and began to climb to a "balcony" about 75 feet above us. My fear of heights didn't kick in because all I could see was 3 feet in front of me or just above my head. When we reached the top, we realized we were in an upper chamber that had been the place of Maya rituals. There were remnants of Maya pottery. The cave was on the property of Cave Branch, and the owner was particular about the preservation of the site. Although we ate lunch in one of the upper caverns, every crumb would leave with us. An adjacent off-limits chamber had an entire wall of crystal that shimmered and glowed in the light from our headlamps. Carol and Martha and I exchanged meaningful glances full of awe and gratitude and amazement. No words were necessary. Very simply, we were the luckiest people in the world.

By 9 a.m. the next day, we had already bused from Cave Branch to Belmopan to San Ignacio and were having breakfast in the rather touristy Eva's Bar. I was suffering in the heat. I had lived in the Northwest for 10 years and was fully acclimated to damp, gray and chilly. I don't do well with sticky and hot. But the excitement of a new place and the natural beauty of Belize took my mind off the fact that my hair was plastered flat to my head and the intense sun preyed on my white Washington State skin.

While researching this trip I tried to make it as varied as possible. The rusticity of Cave Branch was to be balanced out by the more genteel amenities of Duplooy's resort. What a setting! So many strange plants and flowers in the gardens! The site was surrounded by lush mountains and beckoning paths led to a river. It was a birdwatcher's paradise.

The heat grew even more intense until I had to lie down. But lying down didn't help, as I was stifling in the heavy air, feeling that I couldn't breathe. We all went down to the river and swam, which afforded just enough relief to make the rest of the afternoon bearable.

Two days later, we were passengers on a crowded, dusty, Guatemalan bus looking at all the clear-cuts now occupied by cattle and crops. The mini-van from Duplooy's had dropped us off at the border and we connected with the bus that would take us to Santa Elena in the Petén region of Northern Guatemala. I first visited this region with Bob back in 1990, but we had flown in from Guatemala City. This route from Belize was depressing, so much jungle decimated. I knew that people have to earn a living, but the cattle that grazed on the land caused so much damage that within a very few years it had to be abandoned.

Santa Elena was not an attractive place in 1995. It sits on the edge of Lake Petén and a bridge connects it to Flores, a town on an island in the lake. Flores was rather charming although its inhabitants have to deal with the uncertainly caused by the level of the lake fluctuating widely from year to year. My decision to find a hotel in Santa Elena rather than in Flores was because it would be easier to get to the bus station at the crack of dawn a few days hence. The Hotel San Juan faced the lake. We arrived around noon and found our room had yet to be cleaned. The beds had been stripped and cigarette butts dotted the floor. No-smoking rooms had yet to come into vogue. We dropped our backpacks, ate lunch and grabbed a boat to take us to the zoo, which was situated across the lake.

Again my memory of my previous trip didn't jive with the reality. The zoo was now under the provenance of the University of San Carlos and was well maintained, whereas I remembered it as rather shabby. Directly behind and above the zoo was a "resbalada"… a water slide that shot people out into the lake. It was a cement chute with a right-angle turn halfway down. A sign in an amateurish script read "Throw Yourself Off at Your Own Risk." Cultural differences regarding safety issues revealed much … you knew there would be no lawsuits for injuries. There were no officials, no tickets, just the slide. Eric was the first one down and, although we could not see him after he made the right-angle turn, we heard the splash in the water far below. As soon as he climbed the steps to the top, he "threw himself off" again. Not to be outdone, Martha decided to give it a go. But clothes on the concrete chute impeded the "slide factor," and she threw us her blouse. A bra and shorts afforded enough skin for a good, fast slide. She loved it.

I had never been on a water slide. I had to try it because of the new experience and because I couldn't be outdone by Martha. I took off my tee shirt and lay on the cement. And with a whoosh, I was off. It was much faster than I had anticipated and I yelled "shiiiiiit" as I slid around the curve. "Keep your eyes closed," I reminded myself because I was wearing my contact lenses. My eyes were tightly shut as the slide ejected me about 5 feet above the lake like a rather sloppy cannonball. What an adrenaline rush! I was so intent on keeping my eyes closed that I forgot to close my mouth and I took in a good quantity of lake water. My first thought was of pride ... I had done it! The second thought arrived immediately after the first ... it struck me that I could get very sick from the unclean water, but it was too late.

Our boat dropped us back in Flores soaking wet. But we didn't care! We were (Eric excepted) middle-aged daredevils! No ordinary vacation for us! A thrill a day! Before going back to our hotel across the bridge we stopped in a shop that had souvenirs. One look at us and the proprietor queried, "Resbalada, no?" I nodded and grinned. He frowned and shook his head. "You know," he said, "that's a dangerous place. Just two weeks ago a man from Guatemala City flew off the chute and landed in the water, hitting his head on a submerged log. He died. And," he added as an afterthought. "Many people have been seriously injured when they went too fast around the right-angle turn. They have been thrown off into the jungle." At Your Own Risk was clearly an understatement.

Although Carol and I had been to Tikal National Park, the biggest draw for the Petén region of Guatemala, before, we were excited about visiting again with Eric and Martha. This fascinating, extensive archeological site was somehow magical and surreal as it both blended in and stood out from its jungle environment.

- Tikal is one of the largest Maya ruins and was occupied between 200 and 900 AD.

9

- The monuments and temples are impressive, the site is huge, and excavation and discovery continue.
- The tropical rainforest abounds with flora and fauna and thus a visit to Tikal offers an archeological, botanic and biologic experience all at once.

On arrival back to the hotel, we found that neither the water nor the electricity was working, and our room had not been cleaned. We had no choice but to go out to dinner with plastered-down hair and clothing and smelling none too sweet. We sat down to a dinner of jalapeño pizza. My stomach had happily not reacted to the ingestion of lake water and this was a particularly good pizza covered with jalapeños, cheese, corn and avocado. We were exhausted after a day in the heat exploring Tikal. Not only tired, we were extremely sweaty and I felt the days of high humidity and temperatures beginning to chip away at my usually good mood.

Back in our room, our washed out bras and underwear from the night before were still hanging from the now immobile ceiling fan. Eric got full marks here ... not only was he sharing this room with three older women, he had to deal with looking at our underwear circling around over his head like a mobile. On returning to the room after dinner, the power and water were again functioning. We all showered and packed for a very early morning departure.

At this juncture I think it appropriate that I throw in my litany of complaints.

1. The humidity was extreme. Melting was a distinct possibility.
2. Mosquito bites.
3. Abrasions on the underside of my arms from the inner tubes.

4. Heat rash on arms and legs.

5. Swollen ankles, or elephant legs as I like to call them.

6. A cold sore from too much sun.

Carol also had her complaints.

1. She was getting more and more nervous about the next stage of our journey which was, for us, through rather uncharted territory.

2. She had a mosquito bite on her head that was itching like crazy.

3. She was unable to locate a pair of her earrings and was convinced that the hotel maid had stolen them.

So when we left the not-so-great Hotel San Juan at 5 a.m., Carol was on edge and the heat and humidity of the previous week were taking their toll on me.

GUATEMALA AND MEXICO

Eric was at this point going no farther. While we were headed west into Mexico, he would backtrack east to the Belize Cays to spend time scuba diving with his cousin. Up at an ungodly 3:45 a.m., we left the not-so-great Hotel San Juan at 4:15 and walked to the bus station in the dark. Eric's bus left first. Ours was boarding but we sat quite a while before the driver climbed on board and started the motor. Filling the bus with passengers takes precedence over strict adherence to a time schedule. The route between Santa Elena and the border had just recently opened and the road was dirt. The constant potholes made for a very rough ride. Very rough. Martha compared the experience to being in a human blender and I worried that my fillings would vibrate out of my teeth. The scenery was beautiful. The houses we passed were built with poles and thatched roofs. About an hour from our destination of Naranjo, the bus stopped and we emerged to stretch our legs. We noticed a number of people in army-like clothing circulating and were informed that they were guerillas.

Guatemala had suffered a terrible civil war in the '80s. Racism and repression by the government and military resulted in a slaughter of the indigenous people. More than 100,000 were killed, uncountable were tortured and more than 200,000 were displaced, fleeing for their lives. Although much of this had calmed down by 1995, the continuing impunity of the perpetrators of the atrocities and massacres meant that in some areas indigenous guerrilla fighters continued their struggle for justice.

After about 40 minutes, the bus driver and one of the guerillas shook hands and we all re-boarded the bus. Another guerilla followed us aboard and addressed the passengers. Martha and I sat toward the rear and I translated for her. But Carol sat toward the front, didn't know what was transpiring and was obviously more than concerned about it. She kept turning and looking at me, and I nodded at her reassuringly. Short, good-looking and amazingly well-kempt for living in the hills, the guerilla was also well spoken. "I very much regret the impudence of this unscheduled stop for you and any inconvenience that results," he began, "We are guerrillas and we are fighting for our human rights. You know that we are a repressed and beaten people and we are struggling to better our situation. We are also looking for a political 'space.' (At that time the indigenous were not represented in the government.) At times we have needs, and because of this we have stopped the traffic with the town's permission. We don't do anything without the permission of the people. Thank you for your patience, have a good trip, and may you go well."

The bus population responded "Igualmente" (Same to you) as the young man jumped off the bus. I gave Carol the thumbs-up sign and I saw her take a deep breath. The supplies now purchased, traffic resumed and we settled in for the final hour of the journey to El Naranjo. Once there we would have a four-hour wait before the scheduled departure of our canoe for Mexico.

* * *

And now, sitting on the kitchen chairs on the canoe, the breeze on the San Pedro River is downright relaxing. My tailbone is aching from the hours long rough bus ride earlier, but my shoes are off and the ride is smooth. The river is about 150 meters across and we are going through pristine, mostly uninhabited wilderness. Even when the dark clouds approach and we have a bit of rain we don't complain, as the temperature has cooled a bit and the light wind feels good on our faces. We keep noticing how there are no travelers from the United States and no women even close to our ages doing this kind of backcountry travel. On the boat are two French girls, two German girls and one young Spanish woman who had volunteered at a school in El Naranjo.

After a couple of hours on our kitchen chairs, we pull into an immigration office right at the edge of the river. Behind the immigration building is an army installation. There are 10 of us on the boat and the process of getting us from one country to the other is painfully slow. All information is recorded by hand, and a very slow, painstaking hand at that. There is only one bathroom and it is not really functioning, but after the hours on the river we all are anxious to use it. Mexico: the third and last country on this trip. I put my newly stamped passport in my waist belt and go back to the boat.

La Palma is just a dot on the map where the canoe trip comes to an end. As we pull up to the dock, we see only a few rather primitive houses. We have been on the river for four hours. But today's trek is not yet ended. Our final stopping place is the town of Tenosique, not far away. It is easy to find a taxi and we settle down on the seats with satisfied looks, for we know that the longest, hardest day of travel is behind us.

Our taxi driver has the radio on full blast. Unconsciously, my toes tap to the meringue beat. As tired as I am after such a long, eventful day, the music energizes me. My journal notes only fragments of the song, as understanding lyrics in another language with taxi noise in the background presents some challenges. From what I jotted down, the song deals with a young man who went to a dance. When he started to dance, he stepped on some gum. He was trying to impress the girls, but he couldn't do the steps with the gum sticking to his shoe. The quirkiness of the lyrics appeals to me and I find myself smiling.

Once in Tenosique, we find a room that is satisfactory at the Hotel San José. Hot water and "clima"! (air-conditioning). After a quick dinner of enchiladas suizas in the hotel coffee shop, we need no incentive to turn in for the night after our 14-hour travel day. We had informed the desk clerk that we had a rather significant ant problem in the room and they sprayed insecticide while we were at dinner. Neither the smell of the spray nor the idea that we'd be breathing it all night deters us from falling instantly to sleep.

The bus we catch in the morning is super luxurious. It would have been luxurious even if we couldn't help but compare it to the bus on the dirt road in Guatemala the day before. It has reclining seats, air-conditioning and TV. The air-conditioning alone is so seductive that I fantasize about refusing to leave the bus when it reaches its destination. However, we still have one more stop to make before we gain the elevation that will provide the climate change I am longing for. We all want to visit the Maya ruins of Palenque.

The town, also named Palenque, has grown up on the periphery of the ruins. When we descend from the bus, it is unspeakably hot. I can feel my last reserves of civility slipping away. I am exhausted with the heat and it doesn't take much convincing to persuade my friends to cut our stay in Palenque to one day instead of two. We book our tickets to San Cristóbal de las

Casas for the next morning. I console myself because I can now count down the remaining hours of almost unbearable humidity-laden heat.

Palenque and Tikal are probably the most famous and extensive Maya ruins. Where Tikal is wild and almost intimidating as it blends into the jungle, the excavated ruins in Palenque are in a park-like setting. The temples are surrounded by large green grassy areas. We climb the Temple of the Inscriptions, with the steep 18-inch stairs that Maya ruins always seem to have. This imposing monument stands about 70 feet tall, and at the top, my fear of heights alternates with my breath being taken away by the spectacular views. Thank goodness there is an easier descent around the back.

We explore the Palace with its tunnels and excellent carvings. The sweat pours down our faces and our eyes burn with the salt. We don't do Palenque justice because the heat is absolutely oppressive. Ten years later Carol and I would return to Palenque to find it even more refined and its setting even more park-like. As Palenque is easier to access than Tikal, the number of tourists has increased dramatically. On that second visit it was almost too crowded.

Upon leaving the ruins and heading back into town, we agree on our two top immediate goals. Aguas de papaya rate as our number one priority. Mexican papayas are the size of footballs and so cheap. An agua de papaya is just the thing to quench thirst and line your stomach with soothing papaya. Taking a cool shower comes in a close second. Those accomplished, we rest up a bit, improving our moods by reading tourist brochures with hysterical mistakes in the English translations.

Although our alarm is set for 6 a.m., we all wake even earlier. We had opted for the first-class bus for the five-hour ride to San

Cristóbal. It's scheduled to leave an hour before the second-class bus and costs only marginally more. Once again we settle into a luxurious bus. Our attention is divided between the spectacular scenery and the movie replete with sex and violence. About an hour and a half into the journey, the bus loses power and stops. The driver strips off his shirt and makes some adjustments under the rear of the bus. We are advised not to use the bathroom, which was located right over where he's working. The bus starts right up but loses power again in less than a mile down the road. The driver coaxes a few more minutes out of it before it dies completely in the middle of nowhere on a curving mountain road. Off comes his shirt and he crawls under the bus again. The heat inside the bus rapidly becomes stifling and yet all the women and children stay seated, uncomplaining. A number of male passengers gather around the rear of the bus and make suggestions to the driver. Carol, Martha and I get off and float around for two hours on the side of the road … anything to avoid the oven that the bus had become. Two buses stop and their drivers offer assistance. The three of us walk up the road a bit and become human curtains so we can pee one at a time out of sight of the bus. We have to try to gauge for oncoming traffic, which is difficult because the curves in the road cut off our sight.

Amazingly, the driver once again gets the bus going, but not before the second-class bus we had decided against comes chugging along and passes us stalled at the roadside. This is not the first time that I've been on buses where the driver doubles as mechanic. And what is amazing is that, in most instances, the bus ultimately does get us to its destination.

As we drive past Ocosingo on the bypass road, about the halfway mark of the trip, we are again at a standstill, thwarted this time by an electrical cable stretched out on the road like a long snake. A handful of men appear and lift the cable with long sticks while our bus passes gingerly underneath. I am not well versed on electrical matters, but everyone seems intent on the cable not coming into contact with any part of the roof. The men, who are normally short in this part of the world, look even shorter to me as I watch them stretch as high as they can with their sticks to get the cable over the top of the bus. I didn't realize that I have been holding my breath until we hear the "all clear" shout. Whew. We continue the rest of the way without incident, arriving well over two hours late.

SAN CRISTÓBAL DE LAS CASAS: FIRST GLIMPSE

Our triple room is luxurious; the hotel has flowering courtyards and tiled fountains. It's amazing how yellow and orange paint in a room can cheer one up. By the standards on this trip, Hotel Flamboyant is a splurge ... it set us each back $19 per night. But after the hot and sticky trip, we feel justified. I probably should point out again that we are not young backpackers but middle-aged women who are a bit more used to our creature comforts.

San Cristóbal seems quiet. I admit to some ignorance as newspapers in the States don't give more than an inch to rebellions to the south. The town is indeed subdued, still getting its bearings after the small but very meaningful and symbolic revolution that took place the previous year. Eighteen months earlier, the EZLN (Ejército Zapatista Liberación Nacional—The Zapatista National Liberation Army, named after Mexican revolutionary leader Emiliano Zapata) stormed into San Cristóbal and Ocosingo and began a 10-day fight against the Mexican government. The EZLN was comprised of a group of Maya who, in addition to protesting the implementation of NAFTA on New Year's Day 1994, were making their voices heard with regard to civil rights for indigenous people. In El Salvador, Guatemala and Nicaragua, the indigenous were effectively denied their human rights by repressive governments. The recent civil wars in those countries provided a model and beacon for the unrest in the indigenous communities in Chiapas, which were all too familiar with socio-economic inequality. Negotiations between the EZLN and the Mexican government began soon after in San Andrés Larráinzar and over months and years the path to a mutually beneficial peace accord stalled repeatedly. The failure to reach agreement could be attributed to the government's unwillingness to address the root causes of the rebellion and the fact that during the peace talks military bases in the region were fortified. Much paramilitary activity (believed to be government supported) including outright attacks, low-intensity warfare and general harassment, was inflicted particularly against the ELZN- leaning communities. Eighteen months after the initial rebellion, tourists are still shunning San Cristóbal de las Casas and, as per usual after such an event, it will take some years to recover.

We step into a light rain when we leave the hotel the next morning, first in search of a laundry and second for a red umbrella in the main square, the Zócalo. The first task accomplished and our very dirty clothes left behind, we spot the red and white umbrella and under it, Mercedes Hernández, the woman whose tour of the local villages has been highly touted in the guidebooks.

I remember Mercedes with fondness because she introduced me to the indigenous communities around San Cristóbal that opened up my life in ways that were not even conceivable at the time.

Mercedes, herself half indigenous, explained that:

- The town authorities are divided among party officials (at the time the PRI had been in power for decades), the caciques (locally chosen men who serve a "cargo" or town administration post and give public audience, advice and rule on minor crimes), and the religious officials who take charge of the festivals and saints.

- Girls often marry as young as 14 and have 8 or 10 children by the time they are 30.
- Shamans serve a social role in the community by means of their healing and ritual practices.

She is hopeful about the Zapatista rebellion, is "in love" with Bishop Samuel Ruiz, who is facilitating the peace accord talks. She is also "in love" with Subcomandante Marcos, the non-indigenous pipe-smoking man of unknown identity who has become the spokesperson and major communicator for the movement. "All the women are in love with Marcos," smiles Mercedes, "I'll have to stand in line."

Daily, Mercedes leads a tour to both San Juan Chamula and Zinacantán, two communities within 20 minutes of San Cristóbal. She is a one-woman show: entertaining, informative, funny and, having grown up in Chamula, she is known, which is a definite advantage. The tour starts when we descend from the van on the outskirts of Chamula. We stand around three crosses, all painted a bluish green. These are Maya crosses, so identified because the top and the ends of the crosspiece are round. The four spokes represent the four directions. The incoming Spaniards, finding a cross so similar to the Christian cross, realized that they could utilize an existing icon and attribute to it a new, "improved" meaning. Crosses like these are seen frequently in Maya communities. These three in particular represent the three regions of the Chamula municipality. The middle one, the tallest, indicates the "head" region, San Juan, where the church of San Juan de Bautista is located.

Saint John the Baptist wasn't always the patron saint of the town. Not far from the main plaza lie the ruins of the church of

San Sebastian. Although the roof is gone, the four walls and the arched door remain as the pivotal point of the community cemetery. San Sebastian was the first patron saint here. But when the church was destroyed twice by fire, he was deemed insufficiently strong to continue in that position. He was usurped by Saint John the Baptist, who has managed to hold the job ever since. The ruins of the old church lend gravitas to the graves that surround it. Each grave is marked by a colored cross that indicates whether the deceased was young, old, male or female.

In the center of town is the church of San Juan. It's not just a church, it's an experience. I've been there a dozen times and it is never quite the same. I hesitate to describe it because not only does it affect everyone differently, but the rituals and appearance change depending on the date. Suffice it to say that it is one of the most spiritual places I've ever encountered. Think pine needles, candles (thousands), music, incense, ceremony and healings.

The Chamulans, Mercedes informs us, are a proud people who resisted the Spanish influence ever since the Spaniards arrived in 1524. The black wool skirts and the distinctive sateen blouses worn by the women and the white or black wool tunics of the men make the inhabitants of this municipality readily identifiable. San Juan Chamula is a Catholic town that has no qualms about purging itself of newly converted Protestants and sending them packing, usually off to the poverty-stricken barrios on the hills overlooking San Cristóbal or to one of the new towns to the south that have sprung up supported by Seventh Day Adventists or Jehovah's Witnesses.

From Chamula, Mercedes takes us to Zinacantán. Little did I know how much time I'd be spending here in years to come; how at home I'd come to feel in this place. But this initial visit is mainly to see the weaving and embroidery of colorful flowers that symbolize the community. Mercedes' explanations become the subject of our discussions for days to come.

As I wander the streets of San Cristóbal, I find more and more that appeals to me. The Arch of Carmen, built in 1547, is one of the few buildings in Latin America with Moorish architecture. It is connected to the church of the same name that has a tableaux of Saint Carmen complete with a revolving halo and blinking lights. Next to a shrub in the garden outside is a sign that reads "Pellízate la nariz, no mis hojas." (Pinch your nose, not my leaves.) The more I walk, the more I feel that the city is burrowing under my skin.

San Cristóbal was not a travel destination in 1995 and the internet cafes, which in a few years would pop up all over the city center, had not as yet been conceived. The three of us had been basically out of touch with home at all times on this trip. I've traveled alone several times and find that when I internalize the experience, when I can't communicate it, I feel it more deeply. Every time I use the internet, or make a long-distance phone call, I take myself out of the experience and involve myself once again with what is happening at home. As I read my journal, I see that we were totally immersed in the trip in spite of some physical complaints. Martha was fighting a bad cold. Carol was going a bit nuts with the itching mosquito bite she had gotten in Belize. And I had walked into the edge of a door in the dark in our hotel room and had banged my forehead and hurt my ankle, which was swollen and throbbing. None of this distracted from how we felt about San Cristóbal. Rather, we were enthralled by the colors, the weavings, the handicrafts, the setting and the culture. None of us knew that we all would be coming back.

BEST LAID PLANS: 2003

I love planning trips. I love the reading, the research, the arrangements, the anticipation. So when I decided to take a year's leave from teaching and spend three months doing volunteer work in Chiapas, the planning kept me busy for almost a year. I learned, however, that all the planning in the world does not insure success. I also learned that "success" is relative and may not show its face until some time has passed.

My earlier trips to Chiapas were the appetizers. This trip would be the main course. As a teacher, I wanted to help. I saw so much untapped potential among the Maya women. They inspired me. As victims of one of the rawest deals in history going back all the way to the Spanish conquest, they have had to fight against societal woes of racism and sexism. The poverty was abject; the opportunities scarce. Education was lacking; water contaminated; the number of babies dying before the age of 5 was appalling. Regardless, they possessed an unbelievable strength in the face of discrimination. They confronted circumstances so disheartening that giving up seemed the sensible thing to do.

So I decided to spend three months in San Cristóbal, the colonial city in the mountains of Chiapas with a majority indigenous population that I had visited twice before. Until 1994, Chiapas had been a little-known Mexican state. That year the Zapatista rebels staged a small revolution in the name of justice and education and respect for indigenous people. Led by the mysterious, charismatic, mellifluous, pipe-smoking Subcomandante Marcos, the rebellion was welcomed and praised by justice-seeking people worldwide. As a result, the consciousness of indigenous people was raised and indigenous women in particular saw glimmers of opportunity.

I wrangled a letter of recommendation from a human rights' group that I support and from there I was able to get the name of a woman who worked with a cooperative of seamstresses. The e-mails started to fly fast between us. Within a month I had arranged to work with the women in the cooperative as a teacher. Ramona, the coordinator of the cooperative offered me lodging at her house. I was all set. And excited. And nervous. Okay, I need to throw in some disclaimers here. First, I was no spring chicken. I was 55 as I made my plans. Second, I had never volunteered out of the country and by myself before. Third, I have lived a typically American life in terms of conveniences: that is, I own a car, a house, a food processor and I can afford to take my cats to the vet. Fourth, although I had traveled alone several times and had been away from home and Bob for as long as five weeks, three months was going to be a stretch.

I flew from Seattle to Houston to Mexico City to Oaxaca. The route was not the most straightforward, but a retiree of Delta Airlines had gifted me a free pass, and Oaxaca was the closest airport served by Delta. From there I would travel via overnight bus to San Cristóbal. I refused to entertain any thoughts of the travel guides that cautioned against overnight bus travel — especially for women and doubly for women traveling solo. As we pulled away from the bus station at around 8 in the evening, I considered myself lucky to have an inflatable neck pillow and two seats to myself. Both, I realized, were essential. The bus was first class and had the requisite television and bathroom. The darkness and twisty roads produced an almost instant nausea that became acute if I so much as allowed my eyes to look at the movie playing just above my seat. Two hours later, the road straightened out and I dozed off and on until a stop at 3 a.m. allowed a change of drivers and a chance to use a bathroom and grab a small bag of cookies. The next time I awoke, the bus was motionless.

Up until the day before, a hurricane had been pounding the Caribbean coast of Mexico and the winds and rain had traveled well inland. Between the little town of Cintalapa, where we had stopped, and Tuxtla Gutiérrez, the capital of Chiapas, the road had washed out. Now it's hard to believe, but this was the only route. Traffic was queued up in front and behind us, and we all just sat, waiting for some kind of news. I shared this big bus with only nine other travelers, most of them European, one Mexican, and me the only American. Several of us found a small restaurant for breakfast and we swapped the usual travel horror stories. After eating, I returned to the bus and took a nap. And we waited. Rumors flew up and down the line of vehicles. The road would open in half an hour; the road wouldn't open until tomorrow; the bus had to return to Oaxaca; a taxi could take us to the washed-away road and we could walk across and find transportation on the other side. We tried this, and the taxi had to turn around. I found the situation strangely freeing. There was nothing I could do to change the road, or the bus, or the weather. I couldn't clean my house, run errands or make phone calls. I was forced to go with the flow.

At about 10 a.m., the bus driver got word that the road had opened. Among a flurry of returning passengers, the line of vehicles, with their infinitely patient drivers, began to move. For about 15 minutes we went at a good clip, but then we came to a halt. For the next two hours we inched our way forward until we arrived at the washout. The road was indeed gone, but two large metal pipes were left, and one by one, alternating directions, cars and trucks were moving across the pipes, accompanied by the animating cries by a group of men who were orchestrating the movement of the endless line of traffic. I pasted my face to the window to watch as our bus gingerly drove over the exposed pipes.

After that, we made good time to Tuxtla. But once there we saw the heartbreaking aftermath of the storm. Many of the city streets were impassable, either flooded with water or filled with mud. All the existing traffic was routed to a few safe streets, which meant that again we were making almost no progress. The devastation kept me perversely glued to the bus window. People had carted their belongings out to the street to get them out of flooded houses. Big piles of ruined mattresses and furniture lined the water-filled sidewalks. Men and women were still carrying out their possessions, their faces numb as they discarded their belongings.

After a quick stop at the bus station, where no one got on or off, our bus inched its way out of Tuxtla and started the final leg, the climb up the mountain to San Cristóbal de las Casas. A 10-hour trip had turned into a journey of 19 ½ hours. I found a cheap but comfortable hotel, fell into bed, and slept for 12 hours.

I met Ramona the next day. She was the coordinator for the women's cooperative and had offered me lodging for $60 a month. She had a 4-year-old son, Hugo, who like many boys in the machismo tradition, could do no wrong. The house had no living room. There was a toy room with a TV for the boy, but no places for adults to sit. My room was closet-sized, the bed filling almost the entire space. There was a small wooden table and a niche in which I could hang a few clothes. A curtain was my door. The bathroom was modern, tiled, the only drawback being its location down uneven stairs and across the patio. In the night I had to go outside, often in the rain, to get to it. A shower had to be anticipated by lighting the pilot and waiting 20 minutes, which guaranteed lukewarm water for three or four minutes before turning cold.

It was the kitchen that caused me problems. Ramona was no cook. In the two weeks that I was there, I saw her fix quesadillas once and nothing else. The oven top and the broken shelves displayed the burnt remnants of former meals from a former tenant. The kitchen had not been cleaned in recent history. The limited counters were stacked with glasses and fruit and cereal boxes. Dishes were rinsed under cold water with no soap. My gringo stomach had visions of multitudinous bacteria creating comfortable homes on all the plates and utensils. My first morning there I had to scrape the gnats off the papaya. "I can do this," I repeated doggedly to myself, determined not to let this tiny bit of adversity get me down. The condition of the kitchen notwithstanding, I found Ramona to be welcoming and dedicated to her work.

When I first visited Central American countries in the early '90s, the indigenous women left me "boca abierta." (literally, "open mouthed," "amazed.") Women whose husbands had been "disappeared," who saw their children killed, their homes burned. Women who had taken up arms, who had fought for the rights of clean water and basic education, who had stood up to soldiers, who had been put in jail and tortured. Despite the horrors they witnessed, they were not defeated ... no, instead they took action, they formed organizations to continue their struggle and they did so at great personal risk. Many had nothing, only a strong faith and an unshakeable conviction. I, who had had all kinds of opportunities, who could make independent decisions, who had never faced starvation or worried that my son would die of dehydration, was astounded by the strength that I witnessed. Their determination in the face of so much adversity inspired me to action.

Indigenous women are the bottom rung of society. And that's why I wanted to work with them. Maybe I was going in as a "teacher," but I knew that I would learn more than I would teach. The women in the seamstress cooperative came from villages as far as five hours away to attend the workshops held every two months. Some had to walk part of the distance. Some spent hours in crowded vehicles on curvy mountain roads. They hungered for knowledge and for validation. Some attended against the wishes of their husbands. Some said they would never marry because they would lose their independence.

The workshop was held in a three-room house that wrapped around a patio. The women, about 15 of them, slept on the floor. The only room with furniture was the meeting room, filled with a basic table and wooden chairs. There was one toilet for all, which was flushed by pouring a bucket of water into the bowl after each use. Charts lined the walls explaining the daily duties: washing dishes, cleaning the toilet, sweeping the floors, cooking the breakfast. Each woman filled in her name for four days of responsibilities.

The first day was devoted primarily to pattern making. Two women arrived with papers full of measurements. Out came the pattern-making tools: yardsticks and curved measuring sticks. One woman in particular, Margarita, was an expert at this, and a real dynamo besides. She was tireless, enthusiastic and endlessly patient as she moved from table to table, switching effortlessly from Tzotsil to Tseltal to Spanish, explaining how to transform numbers into patterns. And the women worked. The sewing couldn't commence until the patterns were ready.

The next three days were interspersed with seminars. Women who had recently attended classes or workshops shared their information. One session focused on self-esteem, a new concept. The women, not used to speaking in public, still were able to talk about what they were proud of. Most mentioned "el traje," their clothes, as a symbol of who they were. Coming from different villages, the beautifully woven shawls and skirts represented tradition. Another session dealt with "clear communication." About half of the women were illiterate, so when materials were passed out, a lot of time was spent in reading to those who couldn't.

The second morning, I met the women at an internet center and helped them learn the basics of e-mail and introduced them to Google. Many were somewhat familiar with computers, but two months between workshops meant two months between each practice session and much information had been forgotten. I moved from computer station to computer station, explaining the basics. The atmosphere was fun, and yet intense, as the women painstakingly typed and set up e-mail accounts. They showed particular interest in Cancun, wondered what it looked like and where it was because they were aware of the recent World Trade Organization conference that had been held there.

The following morning I headed to the Zócalo, the main plaza of the city. I basked in the bright sun as I made my way to the plaza in front of the Cathedral. The cooperative was participating in a march against both Plan Panama[1] and genetically modified seeds. I was cautioned not to march, as foreigners participating in political activities can be and have been deported. Grandmother Soledad, one of the two founders of the cooperative years before, had also chosen not to march, and she and I

---

[1]   See Appendix for a summation of the current status of the plan.

took up residency on a park bench where we could babysit three children whose mothers were participating. Another demonstration was going on across the plaza, to collect aid for the people of Tuxtla devastated by the hurricane that had delayed my bus. When the young man approached our bench with a can for coins, Soledad had a coin out before I did. Why is it that those who have nothing or little to give, are so quick to share?

Following the march, a group of people listened attentively to a man with a megaphone who expounded on the negative influences of Plan Panama. I crossed the street to listen as well. In a nutshell, Plan Panama, now called the Meso-America Plan, was officially launched in Mexico in 2001 to improve infrastructure and communications and facilitate trade. In reality, the environment and indigenous communities were placed on the sacrificial altar to encourage investment by national and multinational corporations, and to allow for privatization of water and other resources at the expense of the poor. The challenges facing the indigenous loom supernaturally large.

In 2003, Plan Panama was still new. The young man with the microphone called it a betrayal. The government one more time was following the path of money rather than the path of humanity. As the talk continued, my eyes were drawn to the huge map of our hemisphere that served as his backdrop. The map was titled "La militarización estadounidense de las Américas" (the U.S. militarization of the Americas) and included The School of the Americas located in Fort Benning, Georgia. I couldn't believe it. My mind could hardly take in the fact that I was seeing this noted on a map in San Cristóbal. The School of the Americas is well-known for its role in training dictators and military personnel, especially Latin American military personnel, in ways to repress indigenous populations which threaten the financial status quo or the existing power structure of our hemisphere.[2]

I turned to one of the indigenous women next to me in the plaza and asked if she knew what the School of the Americas was. Oh yes, she did, and she told me. I was astounded. When my friend and I had gone to protest there in 2000, I found that few Americans knew about it, and here I was, standing in San Cristóbal next to people who had little education, and they knew. I was humbled.

***

On the home front, I learned how to operate the water heater for the shower. I took my clothes to laundries rather than use the small washing machine and then hang my clothes on the lines across the patio where they were subject to nightly rains. I tried to get the 4-year-old not to push through the curtain that served as the door to my tiny room and get into my things. Although I can speak Spanish, Ramona spoke a fast and furious vernacular filled with unfamiliar idioms and when she spoke I hung on to the conversation by main strength. The absence of a living room meant that when I was in the house I was sitting on my bed, or more rarely, on hard wooden chairs in the kitchen. The alternative was walking around town, passing time in the internet cafes, exploring, sitting in the zócalo or visiting the churches. I walked endlessly.

Thinking that perhaps different living quarters would improve my outlook, I checked out some rental signs. One was for a cottage behind a hostel. It was tiny, without windows, and the kitchen was shared with everyone in the hostel. I checked out an apartment. It was a good size and light, but had no furniture

---

[2]   See http://www.soaw.org/ for more information

and was too expensive just for me for three months. A third option was a dark, dank room in a line of dark, dank rooms. The rooms opened onto a concrete corridor and faced a row of locked doors. These were the toilets. No, I didn't think so. After walking a good mile to another address, I found an apartment that looked as if a bomb had gone off inside. The broken bed frame left at an angle in the middle of the room and a stained broken chair in the corner hid clues to a story I didn't even want to imagine. I'd think about it, I said, backing out hurriedly. And still another lead. A small hotel rented rooms by the month. But no kitchen and no windows.

During all this searching, I was constantly aware of my limited resources. I had saved as much money as I could in the 10 months before I left, but I had to be very frugal. I finally found a small house, not in a particularly convenient location but in a nice neighborhood. It was small, furnished, had a decent kitchen, even a small yard. I was tempted. The rent was $400 per month, which may well have been doubled when they saw me coming. I would have to buy bedding and dishes. I would need to arrange bottled water and electricity. I just couldn't afford it. Come on, I tried the pep talk. You can manage at Ramona's. You'll adjust. Stick with it.

The day after the workshop was over, Ramona and I headed to the town of Las Ollas. This was one of the communities where I would be teaching, and I needed to know how to get there. It's about a 40-minute ride in a colectivo (a taxi shared by as many persons as will fit) up into the mountains. While I should have been captivated by the scenery, the high mountains, the intense blue skies and the corn climbing up the hills, I was mainly conscious of the driver hurtling around the curves on the windy road. Crosses marked the places where the drivers hadn't negotiated the curves, where people had died. The class was to meet at Flavia's house, which was furnished with essentially nothing. Two child-sized wooden chairs were brought out for Ramona and me, while the other women who had joined us sat on the ground. The house was a shack with hammocks and a covered area for the comal, where the tortillas are made. Flavia's 10-year-old daughter was making tortillas and roasting corn. A small milpa (corn field) was behind the house. Ramona and I split the ear of corn we were given. I went to use the latrine, no more than a hole behind the house. It was covered in urine and I couldn't get near it so I peed on the ground.

I started to feel scared. This fear was worse and more all-consuming than the feeling of being overwhelmed that I had been fighting the past two days. I felt so alone. A month earlier I had been so proud, single-handedly arranging this volunteer opportunity. I had felt capable and independent, but now I realized there was no support group. No one with whom to debrief. And my mood swings were unsettling: from confidence to panic. My journal reads "The clouds are rolling in. My clouds are rolling in."

Grapefruit seed extract is a wonderful thing. I found in recent years that two of the bitter drops in water each morning ward off the stomach problems that usually plague me in third-world countries. But even the extract could not protect me after eating the roasted corn at Flavia's, and that night I had to navigate the uneven stairs and run across the wet patio three times. The next day, I spent some time resting and translating a list of the women's products for Ramona, and she made me some chamomile tea to settle my stomach.

I wanted to cut and run, but it was not an acceptable option. Too much planning and anticipating had gone into this volunteer effort. But I had to confess that the doubts were piling up. At the internet café, I found I had 12 e-mails. One was a very supportive one from my son and another was from a friend who was struggling while serving in the Peace Corps in Thailand. She wrote that staying was a daily decision.

Monday was a day for errands. I went to the market and bought a pillow and a hairbrush. I bought thread. I purchased small notebooks and pencils for the women. I walked to the edge of town to the Museum of Maya Medicine and watched a video of a birth. In the film, the fully dressed woman knelt on the floor in front of a chair on which her husband was seated. She put her arms around him for support and held on tight. Behind her was the midwife, who catches the baby. The woman delivering the baby was quiet, and the midwife extracted the baby from within the folds of the mother's skirt. A modest approach.

I sat on my bed, ate a banana and organized a self-esteem workshop. Then I started working on an English lesson. I made a tuna casserole and managed to get the oven to work, after pulling out the broken shelves. I was nervous about tomorrow, my first day of teaching.

I headed off to Las Ollas at about 9 a.m. and arrived about 10. The women hadn't arrived at Flavia's yet, so I watched her daughter make tortillas. Six women participated that day, along with Flavia's 11-year-old son. I had prepared a name game to help me learn names quickly, but as four of the six were named María, the game went by the wayside. They had requested some basic English words to use when selling in the market and I used the "sack" technique that I use in my beginning Spanish classes. I had a number of objects in a bag, or pictures of objects and extracted them one by one, using lots of repetition of the unfamiliar English words. The objects went in and out of the bag as the women started to remember the words. Dogs, pitifully skinny cats, ducks and chickens moved around us. After about two hours of a lot of laughing and fun, one of the women had to leave to attend a meeting about health concerns, so we adjourned. I hitched a ride back to town in the back of a truck.

As good as I felt about my first single foray out to teach, I woke up the next morning extremely sick to my stomach. A nervous stomach. I felt as if everything was horribly wrong. I wanted to go home. I hoped that the busier I got, the more my panicky interludes would abate. On Thursday, Ramona and I were supposed to go to the town of Chenalhó, but we got a call that the half-hour walk at the end of the hour and a half bus ride was dangerous due to mudslides.

That night, unexpectedly, there were several women at the house and long lines for the bathroom. Ramona is generous with her space as well as her time. On my nightly trip to the bathroom, I cautiously stepped over the sleeping bodies in the room adjacent to mine.

I developed lessons. I sat on my bed and filled notebook pages with ideas. And in between I walked, or sat in the Cathedral or the Iglesia de Santo Domingo, or drank coffee and went to the market where the women have chickens hanging upside down from their arms like bracelets. I felt lonely and scared. I walked gingerly because with the rain the smooth stone sidewalks were slick like glass and, sure enough, after a few days of rain, I fell, hard, on my tailbone and landed in the street. At that precise moment, I surrendered to the panic and I sat in the street, crying. A small, middle-aged man ran over to me and picked me up. I felt as if all my reserve had melted away, that I had nothing left. My tailbone ached as it did when I had broken it years before. My wrist hurt. I have never felt such overwhelming panic.

A few minutes later, I was seated in a taco restaurant. I had washed my face and ordered tacos. This panic and this cut-and-run mentality were overshadowing all else. Regardless of the schedule planned for me for the next few weeks, regardless of my commitment to myself, to the women, to many people who had supported my decision to come here, I knew I could not stay. When I even entertained thoughts of staying, the panic rose up in me like bile and the tears came. I shook my head; I had never experienced such fear.

I didn't want to burn any bridges. My sister, who is 20 years older than I am, had been reading my disparaging e-mails and was begging me to return to the States. I walked slowly back to Ramona's, my tailbone aching miserably, and told her that a family situation was causing me to change plans. Family! Ramona understood completely. I donated most of the monies that I would have lived on for the next couple of months to the women. I left piles of notebooks, pencils and other supplies for them as well. Ramona and Hugo accompanied me to the bus station and waited with me until my overnight return bus to Oaxaca pulled out with me on it, crying with both extreme relief and mortification at my precipitous departure.

I slept on the bus and when I awoke at 8 in the morning, we were about two hours east of Oaxaca. I opened my eyes to beautiful mountain scenery and lovely valleys. My self-loathing was buffered by the peacefulness and beauty just out the window.

My desire to go home was so all-consuming that when I arrived in Oaxaca I e-mailed my husband and said I'd be home as soon as I could arrange it. Bob responded quickly, entreating me to wait a bit, to get some rest and see if I felt like staying. After all, he added, El Día de los Muertos (Day of the Dead: corresponds with All Soul's Day and All Saints Day, November 1 and 2) was only two weeks away, and hadn't I always wanted to experience this holiday? Due to a teaching schedule, I'd never had the chance. So I slept well and decided to stay. The three weeks

I then spent in Oaxaca were healing. I found some volunteer work that occupied me for a few days. I spent three days taking advantage of all the activities that I could for El Día de los Muertos. I visited the cemeteries and the flower-laden graves waiting for loved ones to return in spirit. I marvelled at the meticulous sand paintings of saints that adorned the entrances of some of the cemeteries. The huge mounds of yellow cempasuchil flowers in the markets both symbolized the holiday and lifted my own spirits.

When I got home after a five-week, not a three-month absence, I still felt as if I had returned with my tail between my legs. I felt ashamed that I had abandoned my grand plan. Time does heal all wounds, however, and those feelings passed. I found that no one seemed to think the less of me for trying and failing.

A couple of incidents happened in Oaxaca that may or may not have shed light on my panic. First, I went to a small town to have a limpia (cleansing). A limpia is a spiritual practice that rids the spirit of negative energy. I didn't tell the healer why I was there, just that I had been feeling badly. She performed the cleansing with herbs and chants and candles. When she finished she asked me, "Where have you just come from?"

"Chiapas," I answered.

Her eyes got big. "Oh, no, you can't be in Chiapas. Your personality can't handle all the violence that's happened there … it's too much for your spirit. You would have to leave."

I felt a bit exonerated. I wondered, are we sensitive sometimes to intangibles like that? A few days later, a new guest arrived at the house where I was staying. She did not know me or my tale of woe. She walked up to me and placed a slim book in my hands. "I don't know why I bought this, but I found myself paying for it. When I walked in and saw you, I knew the book was for you. Perhaps you can explain it?"

The book was entitled (in Spanish) <u>Witchcraft and Spells</u>. After I told her my "saga," she explained that she was an American living in San Cristóbal. She had heard stories of the women who were trying so hard to better their lives and of the indigenous men who felt extremely threatened by such independent action. She had heard of spells being put either on the women or on the people working with them. "Maybe," she offered, "your panic and flight were precipitated by a spell."

I don't know. It would be easier to blame a spell than my own over-estimation of my ability to adapt readily to a new, challenging set of circumstances. So while those are interesting explanations, I think that I had just bitten off more than I could chew. If I had had a support buddy … if I had had better living conditions … if I had been younger … if I hadn't fallen … the list could go on.

Time passed. My tail emerged from between my legs. I'm still not happy with how fast I left, but I learned a lot. Mainly about me. And that's good. Moreover, unbeknownst to me, a seed had been planted and was just waiting to sprout and grow.

MUJERES DE MAIZ CONCEPTION: 2005

The road to San Cristóbal de las Casas was blockaded just 10 kilometers from the city. Men in traditional dress had dragged logs into the middle of the highway and were calmly sitting on them. My group and I descended from the bus and walked through the stalled traffic. An enterprising man appeared with white cheese, and I bought some to share. It was fresh and cool and crumbled in our mouths. The first taste of Chiapas. As we waited, some handicraft stalls on the side of the road caught our eyes and eventually some of our money.

I was filled with contradictory emotions.

- I was returning to Chiapas after leaving shamefacedly almost two years before and was a bit nervous about how I'd respond to being in a place that I felt had almost literally kicked me out

- I was leading a group of eight people, none of whom had been to Chiapas. I wasn't sure exactly why I was doing this ... but I knew that I wanted others to have the experience of meeting and interacting with the women in the cooperative

- The road blockade would cause us to arrive late for our hotel and I was concerned about our reservations

- The road blockade was a great introduction to the "go

with the flow" Mexican experience

Time passed. Finally I approached some indigenous men who were also patiently waiting and was informed that the blockade had to do with privatization of water. Water rights have become a worldwide issue. Whereas water had traditionally been free to indigenous people in many countries, corporations (Coca-Cola is a case in point) were buying up the rights and charging for usage. This blockade was just such a protest. Four hours after our being stopped, some kind of an accord was reached with government officials and the road was opened.

I had arranged with Ramona to bring my friends to the women's bi-monthly reunion of the women's cooperative. Before we departed the States, I had been thinking of ways to interact and get to know the indigenous women even though we lacked a common language and had radically diverse backgrounds.

Martha R., a friend and art teacher, had come up with the idea of creating a quilt with the women in the workshop. She packed felt squares of many colors and lots of felt that could be cut up. We had glue and scissors and spread all the materials out on the table. Then we asked the women to think of a hope for their community, their country or the world, and make a felt square that somehow illustrated that hope. An hour passed, all of us involved with our quilt piece, and then, one by one, we explained our hope.

Juana hoped that the apple trees would begin to produce like they used to before the use of pesticides in the area. Elena said she hoped people would stop cutting trees. María hoped that the tradition of caring for sheep would continue and Lupita hoped that people would care for the earth. Lucía said she could not read or write and hoped that the girls who came after her would have more education. Other hopes were for world peace, equality between people and less violence. We all were moved. Afterward Martha and Molly started to glue the squares onto a large fabric background. The Hope Quilt was colorful and became a wall ornament for the cooperative for several years until the glued pieces began to fall off.

Getting to know women from another culture, with another language, whose life has been a far different reality, is not simple. And as we went forward with interactive exercises designed to promote understanding, it was some years later that I better understood that such activities are only the preliminary drawings of a bridge that could span such a cultural chasm.

Trust is a huge issue. Later on, after Mujeres had been up and running for two years, Linda (our treasurer) and I were in the mountain community of Crucero talking to the mothers of two girls who had just been given scholarships to start secondary school.[3] The girls were almost 13 and in that rather formless shape between girlhood and adolescence. Their Spanish was almost non-existent and they were painfully shy. One mother bluntly asked us, "So what about next year? And the year after? If my daughter starts secondary school, can she finish?" Her questions reflected centuries of mistrust, of being lied to, of being tricked. "We give you our word," we answered, "We will support your daughter's education for as long as she wants to continue her studies." The mother nodded, hopefully mollified.[4]

According to the Mexican Constitution, primary and secondary education are free. However, secondary education entails

---

[3]   Secondary school in Mexico is the equivalent of seventh to ninth grade in the U.S.

[4]   Frida, the daughter of the skeptical mother, not only finished the three years of secondary school but is now finishing the second year of preparatory (10th to 12th grade). She is running a Children's Program that we support in her community.

a number of add-on fees that make attendance prohibitive for the poor. The cost of uniforms, materials, food for the teacher, photographs, etc. render education beyond the fifth grade a financial impossibility. Many communities don't have

The Hope Quilt
Photo by Martha Rudersdorf

secondary schools. Attendance is thus not only inconvenient but also costly in terms of necessary daily transportation. So the mother's concern was well-placed: She feared that her daughter would suffer disappointment if our promises disappeared after a year or so.

In addition to distrust, the women and girls were so shy. Many did not venture to speak in our presence and when they did, we had to strain to hear them. Our quilt exercise made everyone a bit more comfortable, so we moved on to singing. I taught everyone "Row Row Row Your Boat" in Spanish. After a bit of practice, I notched it up one level and had all of us singing in rounds. When we were finished, the women stood and sang The Zapatista Anthem. Even without understanding the words, the song touched something deep within us and we found ourselves in tears.

That evening found me alternately elated, depressed and feeling a bit anxious. We were learning about another culture in a hands-on way. The ice had hardly been broken, but it was a start. I had the feeling that somehow something was in the offing but my inability to put my finger on exactly what that was made me feel unsettled. I am not a religious person but I am spiritual and I try to honor that which I don't understand. One of my favorite "prayers" that I send out to the universe is to ask that I be open to opportunity and that I allow myself to be drawn to possibilities.

With a heightened energy, we returned to the workshop the next day. The next "getting to know you" activity devised by the women would bring our acting skills (fairly non-existent) into play. We were divided into groups and the women asked us about our lives and daily routines. We explained what we eat for breakfast, what time we go to work, what we do at work (most of us are teachers), how we drive home and fix dinner, etc. Being very aware of how rich we are in comparison to the women, we tried to keep it a bit basic. They then told us of their lives: getting up at 3 a.m. to start grinding the corn, fixing tortillas for breakfast, getting their husbands off to work (usually in a nearby cornfield) and the children off to school. Their house had to be cleaned and swept, any sheep had to be tended, additional tortillas had to be made. Lunch was taken to the husband, clothes were washed, a soup was made. After dinner and all chores were finished and everyone was in bed, usually by 9 p.m., the women finally found time to sew and weave their clothing and handicrafts. An 11 p.m. bedtime afforded them four hours of sleep before the process began all over again.

Hearing each others' daily schedules was just the first part of the activity. We now had to act out their daily routine and they acted out ours. This was all accomplished with much laughter and imagining of details. The acting also reinforced their routine into our memories. We couldn't get over the few hours of sleep, the constant work, the repetition day after day.

A second activity was handled with great discretion. The women had questions about our lives and the questions were a bit sensitive. To ensure anonymity about the authors of these questions, they were written on pieces of paper and put in a container. We all marched around the table to music until the music stopped and the person nearest to the container chose a folded piece of paper and read the question. "Do you have racism in your country?" Several of us answered, drawing on personal experiences, the history of slavery in the South and the on-going controversy concerning immigration policies. A few women looked surprised and others nodded, relating what we said to their own experiences.

Other questions included, "How big were our milpas (cornfields)?" We explained that none of us had an individual milpa.

"Did we have drugs in the U.S.?" (yes, indeed, we did.) The questions and answers captured everyone's interest and engendered further discussion and clarifications. Although many women were painfully timid and others needed translation into Spanish from the Maya languages, communication was open and honest.

After the activities, we had time to observe how the bi-monthly reunion was organized. The representatives from about 10 communities made the trip to San Cristóbal de las Casas every two months. While one community was only 20 minutes away, another was four hours in a combi and a two-hour walk up a mountain road. The women started gathering on Thursday and the actual activities started Friday morning and ran until Sunday evening. Pasted on the walls were large charts with times for workshops, meals, visits to an internet café, all interspersed with rest periods. Another chart listed the chores that needed to be tended to over the course of the three days ... cooking, cleaning the toilet, sweeping, etc. ... with times and days where the women could put their names. Every woman volunteered and thus contributed to the flow of the workshop.

After our activities were finished, we stayed and remarked at how smoothly the workshop proceeded. I sat and made awkward conversation with several of the women, finding them shy to the point where their voices could hardly be heard. They avoided eye contact with me. Iliana was shy, too, but told me she was in school. She loved her English class and wanted to continue studying English at the university level. Later, Ramona told me that Iliana is one of four sisters with a widowed mother and that she worked hard both at home and at school. Her dream of school never strayed far from my thoughts.

PART II

GETTING THERE (LITERALLY)

LONG DISTANCE RELATIONSHIP

Almost everyone I know does some kind of volunteer work. And that volunteer work almost always is close to home. No matter how small the local scene, there are those who take on tasks to help others. This is a wonderful thing. Our group, on the other hand, works in Mexico ... and not Mexico City or one of the easy-to-get-to resort cities. No, we work in San Cristóbal de las Casas, in the center of the highlands in the southernmost state. Because of the long commute that requires hotel stays at the airport both coming and going due to inconvenient flight times, I find a lot of time to jot notes, observations and frustrations in my journal.

For the past few years I have traveled to Chiapas at least twice a year. Linda has always accompanied me during the summer trips when we attend the August workshop of the cooperative and award scholarships, take care of business, visit communities, etc. In December I enjoy leading a small group. It's an "excuse" to visit the women again and to introduce friends and acquaintances to the work *Mujeres de Maiz Opportunity Foundation* does as well as to the region. Other board members come as they are able.

The following are notes from my journal about the "commute."

PERSONAL REFLECTIONS EN ROUTE TO CHIAPAS: 2011

Dan was late and we couldn't leave without him. He had found himself in a 20-mile-long traffic jam en route to the Phoenix airport. Our entire plane full of people sat patiently and waited for Dan, the navigator for our flight. The extra half hour meant I had lost my chance ... admittedly a long shot ... for an earlier flight from Mexico City to Tuxtla Gutiérrez, the capital of Chiapas. I resigned myself to the five-hour layover in the Mexico City airport.

But I had an ace up my sleeve. I had a free visit to an airport priority lounge where I'd be able to rest in comfortable chairs and, in my fantasy, breathe deeply of a luxurious, calming, un-airport-like ambience.

Once Dan arrived, the plane took off quickly. The flight was full. The young girl next to me had never flown before and, although she had a Mexican passport, it was her first time going to Mexico. She was totally bilingual but the customs forms were beyond her. She'd never heard of customs, she didn't know what a "surname" (or "apellido") was, and she didn't know the baggage was stored in a compartment under the plane. She embodied a pure innocence untouched by worldly details.

I dozed off and on. As soon as I landed in Mexico City I started scouting for the priority lounges. There were three. When I couldn't find them I realized that they were located inside security at Gates, F, G and H. My gate was B ... no lounge for me.

What I liked about Mexico City airport (focusing on the positive rather than on my lounge disappointment and the five-hour layover):

1. *Many airport employees were in wheelchairs*
2. *There was a good selection of reasonably priced food*
3. *And OK, there were two Starbucks*

Going with the flow is a Mexican trait to which I aspire. So here I sit, letting go of my airport lounge expectation and enjoying my latte.

TRAVELING WHEN SIXTY-PLUS
APRIL 1, 2011

This will be my 13th visit to Chiapas and it's different. For one thing it's a short visit ... only nine days. I am not schlepping toothbrushes, backpacks or laptops donated for our scholarship recipients. I am not leading a group. I don't have much "Mujeres" business to attend to. I am here for Semana Santa. It's been four months since my last trip. Not long, true, but San Cristóbal de las Casas calls me. I am treating myself to my favorite hotel. It's not expensive, mind you, but family run, friendly and welcoming.

I can't escape the neck pain I've had the past six months but I can get my mind off it. The constant pain has been getting me down, so this trip is just for me.

At this point I have been up since 2 a.m. I am more than tired. Traveling solo is something I highly recommend, but as I get older the whole travel scene becomes more tedious.

ADVANTAGES OF TRAVELING ALONE

1. I strike up conversations more readily with strangers.
2. I do what I want when I want.
3. I speak Spanish all day.
4. Experiences are heightened.

DISADVANTAGES OF TRAVELING ALONE

1. I can't go to the bathroom without maneuvering my carry-on and backpack into the stall with me. Contortions are

often required.

2.   *Anything I purchase I have to carry home. No foisting off items or sharing the weight or volume with husband or friend.*

3.   *The long layovers are a drag (unless you leave from Gates F, G or H and have a priority pass for a lounge.) Right.*

And now we have the AIT machine. The newest security measure, which pictures you sans clothing, has been determined to be safe. How many medications/x-rays/cigarettes were doomed safe until they weren't? I am what they call an "opt-out," which seems to elicit rather unappreciative looks from the security staff. Let me rephrase: I receive almost eye-rolling looks of contempt. A woman is called to pat me down. I can't keep my eye on my luggage, tickets and shoes, which have gone through the x-ray tunnel.

"Wait, wait, my belongings are behind that machine and I need to be able to see them. My life is in those bags," I end with what I hope is a winning smile in the direction of the nearest TSA official. He shrugs and won't meet my gaze. After all, an "opt-out" is a disruption to the assembly line of shoeless, coatless passengers who are slowly but steadily progressing through the security hoops. No sympathy for me. Can't see your bags, dearie? And whose fault IS that?? In a few minutes I see a woman agent approaching and I am taken aside and told in no uncertain terms what she is going to do to me. I think of my next meal or my kittens at home while the agent's gloved hands travel quickly over quite a bit of my body. After her hands are then tested for explosive powder that theoretically came from my clothes, she checks my carry-on one more time and I am free to go.

Another difficulty is that SeaTac, the nearest airport to home, is three hours away and the majority of my flights depart at 5 a.m. For many years I was able to stay at Carol's house, just 25 minutes from the airport. Because she traveled with me often and I was the "trip arranger," she generously would drive me to the airport and pick me up even when she wasn't accompanying me. Two years ago, Carol was diagnosed with ALS and her travel days are over. She's had to move. She's lost her voice and much mobility and is displaying an amazing dignity and good humor in the face of this disease. Due to the change in her circumstances, now a hotel must be booked before early morning flights and after late night arrivals. Time and expense are added to the journey. The travel has become a means to an end, no more, no less. The 18-to 20-hour commute, replete with endless layovers and flight problems, requires more and more recovery time. The trips get longer as I build in more naps.

But I won't surrender yet. Too many places to go. And for the first time, I see an end in sight to the travel and that makes me want to continue the adventures while I still am able.

WHAT CAN GO WRONG JUST MAY GO WRONG

July ??, 2009

It's always a bit frantic just before a trip, but so far getting ready for this one was proving even more challenging. What's with this packing business anyway? I hate to be sexist in any way, but my husband packs about an hour before we leave. I start thinking of what I'm taking a week or so before and I know for a fact that Linda starts virtually packing her suitcase as she lies awake in the wee hours of the night as much as a month before the trip. (More than a month, she admits.) The temperature in San Cristóbal can be cool to warm and in the summer the thundershowers are torrential, so packing everything in a small bag takes some thought.

First, I take clothes I can afford to lose. I hit Goodwill and the thrift shops looking for "disposable" blouses. Second, I take as little as possible. It's easy to drop clothes at a laundry at 9 a.m. and have everything clean by 2 p.m. So, ideally, three outfits should suffice for a two-week trip. Third, I want to carry my suitcase with me for all the obvious reasons, so it must fit in the plane's overhead compartment. And fourth, any extra room is space for items to be brought home and included in our dinner/auction, a Christmas bazaar or the Sequim Lavender Farm Faire.

The week before Linda and I left was a difficult one for me personally. Shirley, my 75-year-old sister, died of Alzheimer's. Although she lived in the Midwest and we were never close, it was a wrench. Second, my son told me he was an alcoholic. The good news was that he had already been sober for more than a year, had completed an outpatient rehab program and was attending AA meetings. Regardless, I had never suspected and my worry for him was keeping me awake nights.

That same week I started feeling rundown and extremely tired. The day before we left, I had chills and my joints ached and I developed a rash. The H1N1 flu epidemic was making headlines and Mexico was reeling from all the bad press. My doctor told me to come right over and took one look and said I had parvo virus. "But," I protested, "I don't have a dog. Doesn't that have something to do with dogs?"

I learned that parvo is one of the most common childhood diseases, right after measles and chicken pox. It's a 14-day virus. My cheeks were bright red with "slapped cheek syndrome," one of the telling symptoms of parvo. Once the rash appears (it was on my arms), the half-way point of the course of the illness has been reached and the patient is no longer contagious. (I didn't know I had been contagious.) Relieved to know that in a week this would be gone, I was determined not to let it interfere with the trip.

In addition to my carry-on bag, I was lugging a bigger suitcase filled to the brim with toothbrushes, toothpaste, solar lights and various and sundry other items for the women of the cooperative. Naturally this oversize bag had to be checked. At the Mexicana counter in the Seattle airport, the agent weighed the bag and checked his screen. He frowned. Not a good sign. My stomach did its customary lurch when confronted with either a potential problem or bad news. Or both.

He said something in Spanish that I did not hear but Linda obviously did as her face went from calm to concerned in a flash.

"What?" I asked.

"He said we were supposed to have flown yesterday."

"That's impossible. The date on our e-ticket is today," I responded quickly checking the ticket one more time. It indeed had today's date.

"I'm sorry," said the agent, "your departure date was yesterday." He still hadn't looked at my e-ticket, only at his screen.

"How is it possible that my ticket says today and your screen says yesterday?"

He shook his head and then went into one of those scrunched brow looks while typing for several long minutes. He couldn't deny that our ticket was for today. We had to fly, as our sub-sequent flight from Mexico City to Tuxtla Gutiérrez was also today. We stood there, exchanging worried looks for several minutes. Finally he told us that we could fly today … there were two open seats. Mine ended up being in front of the toilets, and the incessant flushing would provide background music for the five-hour flight. "Oh, and by the way," he added, "the plane leaves at 9 a.m., not 9:30." We hadn't been advised of that either. Relieved just to be going, we settled in for the otherwise uneventful flight.

Upon arrival in Mexico City (referred to as DF … Distrito Federal), we were handed swine flu questionnaires. I really try to be honest all the time, but I knew that if I checked "yes" to some of the questions I would be detained and possibly quarantined. They might not want to accept my parvo diagnosis, which indeed shares some symptoms with the flu, such as joint pain and headache. So I ticked off the ¨NO¨ boxes that were opposite the list of symptoms.

I pulled both bags, my carry-on and the bigger one, through customs to the sky-train, which would carry us to the other terminal. Walking with both bags was cumbersome due to the weight of the larger bag. We sat in the waiting area of the train for the few minutes until the train arrived. The train had no more than pulled out of the station when I realized, horrified, that I only had one bag with me. When I had jumped up to board the train, my usual habit of pulling only one bag had kicked in. The ride to Terminal 1 takes about 10 minutes and as soon as we arrived, I handed my bag to Linda, told her to wait right there and re-boarded the train for the reverse journey. When I got off the train in Terminal 2, I spotted my bag immediately. It was no longer by the bench but instead in the middle of the room, guarded by a security officer. I was almost weak with relief, delighted to see my bag under the care of an official. I hurried over and started to reach for my bag, explaining that I had forgotten it, when I was told "No se acerque más a la maleta. No la toque."

I couldn't approach any closer nor could I touch the bag to show them my identification tag. By this time a second security officer was on the scene. Because this was a "left" bag, I was informed we had to await the arrival of the "policía federal." The two guards checked my passport. We stood there and made some small talk, and I made sure I was not confrontational in any way. I asked if I could call or get a message to Linda in Terminal 1, and was refused. About 30 minutes passed and the policía federal arrived. He took one look at me and I could see that he was not overly concerned.

"Please approach your bag and open the luggage tag." I was inwardly grateful I spoke Spanish, as none of the three spoke English. I opened the tag and the name was compared with my passport. Whew, I was cleared. They noted the information for my continuing flight, and I told them our airline was Aviacsa and our departure time. They said they would be checking to make sure this bag was still with me when I checked in for that flight.

Onward. Back to Linda, where we congratulated each other on having a 4-hour layover. We were still relaxed knowing we had 2 ½ hours before the next flight. But the Aviacsa counter was ominously quiet. About eight agents were there and only one client. The agent informed us that operations of Aviacsa had been suspended two weeks earlier. Obviously the officials who handed over my "left" bag were unaware of Aviacsa's demise.

"Don't worry, Señora," intoned the agent, "you'll receive a full refund. All you need to do is complete the form on the website." He gave us vouchers for Mexicana or Interjet that would get us a cheap fare. We headed off quickly toward the Mexicana counters. After explaining our situation to the agent, we learned that the last flight to Tuxtla had just closed and there hadn't been any open seats anyway. And compounding the bad news, we were informed that they had stopped honoring the vouchers the day before.

On to the Interjet counters, sweating now, with the strain of pulling both suitcases at a rapid pace. All flights were filled until Friday. This was Tuesday. We had to attend the women's bi-monthly workshop on Friday. A three-day delay just wasn't going to work. I left Linda with the cases and went from one end of the airport to the other to check on buses to San Cristóbal but all I could get was conflicting information. I did know that the trip took at least 14 hours but I wasn't able to ascertain from which terminal in the city the buses left nor could I find out departure times.

I had been holding up pretty well but the combination of frustration, running around and parvo was doing me in. Back we traipsed to Mexicana. They could get us on a flight for Thursday, so we bit the bullet and sprung for the full-fare tickets, after which I called Roberto, our friend/driver in Chiapas, hoping to catch him before he left for the airport in Tuxtla Gutiérrez to pick us up. Calling long distance from a pay phone is a hassle. First I had to buy a phone card and then try to figure out what numbers must be included when I dialed. If you are calling a cell phone from out of the area, the preceding numbers change. Roberto's number wasn't working. Finally I reached his brother who said that Roberto was already en route to the airport. A good part of that hour and a quarter journey is not within cell phone coverage. His brother assured us that he would keep trying to contact Roberto and would relay our new arrival time two days hence.

About this time, an elderly taxi driver spotted our tired, vexed faces and led us to his cab. I wanted him to take us to Hotel Catedral, but he talked us out of it ... a good thing because when I checked that hotel the following day, it was completely full. Instead he took us to the Hotel Plaza Madrid, reasonably priced and with an adequate room. This is a hotel primarily for Mexican families and we were the only gringas in evidence. By now it was about 8 p.m., so we pulled ourselves together and ventured out a block and had a late meal. My rash had now spread to my face and legs and I congratulated myself on having visited my doctor. At least there was one thing I didn't have to worry about.

On Wednesday morning we had quite a comprehensive buffet breakfast included in the price of the hotel. Linda loves "urban hikes," so we set off for the Zócalo, the biggest plaza in the city, about an hour away. I waited while Linda took the tour of the roof of the cathedral, something I'd done a few years earlier. It afforded a wonderful view of the cathedral bell, the Zócalo and the surrounding city.

Those of you who have taken trips with a friend, even a best friend, know that travel can sorely try friendships. Travel involves flexibility, handling stress and compromising your routine. Linda and I taught at the same high school for 15 years. Interestingly enough, I didn't know her well when I invited her to come to Chiapas with me in 2005. After I extended the invitation, a couple of months went by and finally I asked her what she had decided.

"I'm sorry," she began, "I can't go because of the snakes."

"Snakes? What snakes?" I was baffled.

"Well, aren't there a lot of snakes in Chiapas?"

I admitted that I had never heard of nor seen snakes.

"Oh," was her reply, "Then I guess I'll go."

This turned out to be a great decision for both of us as now we travel together every summer to San Cristóbal de las Casas. She is cool in airport snafus, happy in whatever situation she finds herself, yet insistent that I make all arrangements. And, whether it be attending to business of the board or traveling, she is always a good sounding board for me.

After having lunch in a second-story restaurant that allowed us a great view of the Zócalo, we took an alternative route back, detouring to La Ciudadela, a huge handicrafts market where we purchased some great Day of the Dead tee shirts for our auction. Walking affords such a different view of a city. We stopped in churches, saw architectural details not visible from a vehicle and just enjoyed the fresh (well, maybe not fresh but not too bad for Mexico City) air. We must have walked five miles. After an hour or so of rest and writing, we went out for dinner and turned in for an early night.

The next morning, packed and with a taxi waiting, Linda descended to the lobby. I was a couple of minutes behind her and entered the empty elevator. I pressed the button for the lobby and the elevator began its slow descent and then it stopped between floors. Due to a similar experience in an open elevator in France when I was 8 years old, being stuck in an elevator is one of my nightmarish fears. I took a deep breath and pushed the lobby button again. Nothing happened. Maybe a minute later, just before full-blown panic set in, the elevator creaked and descended to the lobby. The taxi ride to the airport, the ensuing flight to Tuxtla and the two-day-late arrival in San Cristobal posed no further problems. We had to admit that the old adage "lemons to lemonade" was valid, and we had enjoyed our Mexico City "surprise."

Postscript: Upon arriving home, I filled out the request for refund on the Aviacsa website. I received neither a reply nor a refund.

PART III

ACCLIMATING: THE JOYS AND THE PAINS

NOT A DECISION

Many years ago when I was teaching high school, a group from Seattle made the rather long trip to Sequim to put on an assembly for the student body. Their main objective was to help teenagers be responsible in situations involving peer pressure and respond with good, responsible decisions. This particular assembly stands out in my mind because one of the performers was openly gay. Now Sequim is a rather conservative community and I truly think that if our principal at the time had been aware of the fact that one of the actors was gay, the group would not have been invited. At the end of the assembly in a question-answer period, a student in the audience made a deprecating comment directed at the gay actor.

As the students filed back into my classroom, I heard a girl remark, "That is so disgusting. How can people decide they want to live a gay lifestyle?"

I motioned for her to come up to my desk and asked her, "So when did you make your decision?"

She looked perplexed. "What decision?"

"You know," I continued. "The decision to be heterosexual. I would think that you'd remember a rather major decision like that."

"I didn't make any decision," she said, "this is just how I am."

"Then, why, "I persisted, "Do you think that someone who is homosexual did?"

She looked a bit unnerved, and then annoyed, and went to her seat. I waited that evening for the phone call from her parents and was surprised when it didn't come.

My working in Mexico with the women of the cooperative reminds me of that exchange with my student. There was no decision to work in Mexico. It just was.

Working within a culture different from one's own holds challenges, surprises, foot-in-mouth situations and laughs. There's a definite learning curve. Some things aren't immediately obvious, and there's no one to take you aside and put you straight.

For example, I attended the cooperative's bi-monthly reunion many times. I'd enter, greet the group as a whole, smile warmly at the women, and then sit down. Three or four years passed before I realized that I should have greeted each woman, kissed her cheek and made an individual comment just to her. Now I do that.

HOME BASE: SAN CRISTÓBAL DE LAS CASAS

Because access to everything a visitor needs lies in the historical center of the city, it's easy to forget that the population of San Cristóbal is over 200,000. There is no accurate count due to the constant instream mainly of indigenous people who are exiled from their Catholic communities because they converted to a Protestant sect or because they practiced a traditional Catholicism as opposed to a Maya Catholicism typical in some communities. Many times literally driven out of their homes, the new arrivals construct and inhabit very poor barrios on the outskirts of the city and up the slopes of the surrounding hills.

The "San Cristóbal" part of the name is for the patron saint of the city, Saint Christopher. The "de las Casas" is in honor of Bartolomé de las Casas (1484-1566), a Dominican who fought against the atrocities committed against the indigenous people of the Americas by the Spanish colonists. He is sometimes thought of as the "father of liberation theology" and was an activist for human rights.

The center of the city, with its two long walking streets, is very attractive and tourist-friendly. Critics feel that the colorful and clean streets with coffee shops and now, French bakeries, give a wrongful impression to the traveler. "There is too much division between what the town *looks like* and the *reality* of living here," commented a person from a local NGO. And it's true. The indigenous are seen in their beautiful traje, their daily wear consisting of a woven shawl and colorful embroidered blouse. The eye-catching clothes are set off by shiny black hair and a smile. Assumptions made on the basis of incomplete information can lead to the myth of "idealized poverty." The truth, that they return at night to the house with the dirt floor and the latrine in the cornfield, is hidden from visitors who stay in the city. But San Cristóbal wants and needs tourists, and so the buildings will be freshly painted and the walking streets extended. Due to the hurricane in Cancún a few years ago, the flu epidemic and the constant media coverage about the violence attributed to the narcotraficantes, tourism has suffered terribly in Mexico. And the downturned economy compounds the tourist "boycott."

Most visitors to San Cristóbal currently are Mexicans who are vacationing within their own country. The city has always attracted young Europeans, especially those who come by way of Cancún, but my impression is that there are fewer these days. Americans are afraid to go to Mexico after reports of the many murders of young women came out of Juarez (on the U.S. border) and the drug-related violence in Michoacán and Acapulco. I live two hours away from Seattle, and there are areas of that city in which I wouldn't walk alone after dark. But that doesn't mean I don't visit Seattle. A few years ago there was a huge teacher strike in the city of Oaxaca and the army was called in and people were hurt and jailed. A friend of mine who lives there said the violence was confined to a few square blocks and as long as one stayed clear of that area, there was no problem. But the press coverage wasn't clear on the limits of the violence and the entire city economy, much of it linked to tourism, suffered for years because potential tourists feared for their safety.

For many Americans, Mexico consists of two coasts, each with big resorts and great beaches, connected by what … desert? … they aren't really sure. Our geology and history classes in high school barely mention Mexico and usually ignore the rest of the hemisphere to the south as well. Every time I head to Chiapas, I get the same two questions over and over.

"But, is it safe?" and "Wow, how do you stand the heat?"

"Yes" I respond to question number one. I walk alone through the streets of San Cristóbal at night without worry and go by myself to outlying communities via public transportation without a thought. Common sense, no matter where one is, is the rule. As to the second query, San Cristóbal and most of the communities I visit are in "Las Altas," the mountains. San Cristóbal itself is at almost 7,000 feet and the climate is temperate.

San Cristóbal has a duality that I experience every time I am there. There is a feeling of being home, a tranquil feeling of belonging. But there is also an external energy, a joie de vivre, which assails the senses with color and noise and exuberance. I am conscious of being more aware of what and who's around me; of being in tune. Within a few days, no matter what time of year, I've seen processions, protests, dance, exhibitions and music … something for all the senses. In no way do I want to make this into a guidebook chapter, so let it suffice to say that excellent restaurants abound, accommodations of all types and prices are plentiful, and it's a perfect place to absorb a fascinating history and culture.

Am I prejudiced? Well, of course, but justly so. With *Mujeres de Maiz Opportunity Foundation*, I usually travel to Chiapas twice a year. The trip I just completed was my 14th and yet, every time I book my next flight, I still feel the same excitement and anticipation. I am doubly blessed to work with the amazing women of the cooperative and to spend time in a place that seeps into my very soul.

To present a balanced snapshot of the city, the following could be perceived as either "obstacles" or "challenges" depending on what type of traveler you are.

- First, the sidewalks are treacherous: uneven and holey, there are metal loops to watch out for, or equally dangerous protuberances. Sidewalks can be high (I know of one that is about three feet off the street) and narrow (I'm thinking of one about 12 inches in width.) But the most risky time is walking when they are wet. Many sidewalks are made of stone that becomes slippery as banana peel in the rain. I have fallen. In each group I have led, there has been at least one fall. Thanks to the universe, no one has experienced a serious injury but one woman last December sported quite the black eye for several days.

- English is not widely spoken. Actually, unless you run into an American ex-pat or a European polyglot, it's rare to find an English speaker. This puts a lot of people off. Go anyway, I say. True, you will have to struggle a bit to be understood, but that's part of the traveling experience: Get out of your comfort zone. I traveled alone in the old Yugoslavia without a word of the language and son Eric and I toured Tunisia and Turkey with a vocabulary of "thank you" and "hello." A smile and friendly manner are all that are needed.

MEXICAN COLOR

Last week, Jack, an ex-pat living in San Cristóbal, and his wife, Rocío, arrived for dinner at our house in Sequim. Jack and I had exchanged a few e-mails in the early 2000s about some weaving and photography tours he was running in Chiapas. I contacted him again when I wanted someone to talk to my group about living there and about the textile tradition. Jack consented and so in 2008 I met him for the first time. When I found out that his son lives in the same small town as I do, I shook my head in amazement. I don't believe in coincidences. I think things are confluent for reasons that may or may not be apparent.

In 2010, I was in Chiapas by myself over Thanksgiving, preparing for the December group I was to lead. Jack invited me to his annual dinner for about 70 people. And when we needed someone to film footage for our *Mujeres'* video, Jack came through for us. Jack and Rocío had now come to Sequim to meet their new grandson for the first time.

Rocío came into our house and her first words were "Estoy en mi casa." ("I am at home.") Our house is rather a riot of color and folk art. I have sponged terracotta colored walls, a cobalt blue and yellow wall, multi-colored woven rugs from Teotitlán del Valle and Santa María del Valle near Oaxaca. I've collected weavings, paintings, clay figures, Huichol bead art … and the bright, primary colors are all represented. I don't have pastels and there is little white or beige. Houses in Mexico tend to be colorful inside and out. One of my first landmarks in San Cristóbal was a huge purple house on a corner.

Here in the Pacific Northwest one of the most common reasons for depression is the lack of sunlight. For me, the lack of color leaves life somehow drained of energy, and all right, I'll confess, boring. Color stimulates me. It charges up my senses. When I look around my house, I feel inspired and content. So Rocío's comment made sense to me. She arrived and saw my house full of the designs and color of her own home and tradition.

In April, 2011, I made a rather impulsive trip to San Cristóbal for Semana Santa. I had never experienced Holy Week there. The morning after I arrived, I walked to the newer walking street, Real de Guadalupe, which is lined with shops and res-taurants. I stood there a bit in shock when I realized that all the brightly painted buildings were now white. The street looked ghostly and uninviting. Although full of Holy Week visitors, the warm, engaging hues were gone.

I soon learned that the ubiquitous white was only primer. Some months later the colors would reappear and the street would awaken anew. Immediately it occurred to me that the current tourists, some who had never visited before and would never again, will forever have in their memory — and their Picasa file — photos of this white street and think that this is how it is, washed out and uninspiring.

Color combinations on the outside of houses may be subtle or bold or even jarring. But the result is that the houses, inside and out, have personality. Many times I've had to stop and dig in my pack for my camera to take a picture of a particular door (the one painted hot pink and lavender is still my favorite) or an unusual or unique color theme on a house.

The impressive white government building, which lines the west side of the Zócalo, is bathed in colored lights at night. For a few minutes it gleams in mint green, then changes to rose, then violet, then yellow. I love seeing the building transform into a rainbow after dark.

The colorful buildings serve as a backdrop for the colorful dress of the indigenous women. The weavings, which translate into clothing, are a feast for the eyes. The embroidery and cross-stitch on the hand-woven cloth are not only incredibly fine work but display enviable individual creativity. San Cristóbal and its inhabitants provide constant eye candy. Linda and I carve out a bit of time some afternoons to sit on the Real de Guadalupe and savor a cappuccino at El Tostador. We bring with us the little paper bag that contains the still-warm pan de chocolat from the Ooh La La Bakery. We sit and rest and relish the passing color. I sigh contentedly. I am home.

RACISM

Scene 1:

I'm in a taxi heading out to the house where the women's bi-monthly meeting is being held. It's my first exposure to the cooperative and to the women, and I am both excited and nervous. The taxi driver asks me where I am going because obviously I am heading out of the part of town frequented by tourists.

"I am going to work with some indigenous women," I reply, keeping my answer short and not giving much any detailed information.

The driver persists, "And what are you going to do?"

"I'm planning to give some workshops," I answer, hoping the vagueness of my response satisfies him. It seems to, because instead of asking me for more information, he decides to fill me in.

"Well," he says, "You know you won't have much success with that. Indigenous people are like children ... even teaching them right from wrong is impossible."

Scene 2:

I made the acquaintance of a 30-something elementary teacher. She teaches in the public schools. During lunch one day, she tells me how lucky she is not to be teaching indigenous children. My frown lets her know that I don't understand her reasoning, so she adds, "Indigenous children are just so dirty. I really wouldn't want to have to have them in a classroom."

Scene 3:

Linda and I had taken two taxi-loads of girls and women to the optometrist for eye exams. When we finished, the women intended to return to their workshop while Linda and I were debating whether we would look for auction items in the indigenous market for our October fundraising event or return to our hotel. The main streets in San Cristobal are practically wall-to-wall taxis just waiting for the merest gesture or glance to carry you to your destination. The women stood in the street as empty taxi after empty taxi drove by. Linda and I watched speechless, feeling more and more uncomfortable. Finally Linda could stand it no longer and she stepped into the street and hailed a taxi. It stopped immediately and Linda opened the door and the women jumped in. When Linda shut the door without getting in, the taxi driver was aware of her "bait and switch" tactic. Defeated, he drove away, his taxi full to the brim. Linda waited a minute and did it again with a second taxi.

Scene 4:

"We are very aware of racism," Veronica enlightened us. "Many times when we walk down the sidewalk, the people won't let us pass. We have to step into the street to avoid being pushed off the sidewalk."

LOS TAXISTAS

Living on the Olympic Peninsula is wonderful. The natural beauty of mountains and water lend a quality to life that cannot be duplicated. But what we lack is a system of public transportation that takes us where we want to go, when we want to go, on the cheap. Living here without a car is difficult, almost impossible.

On the other hand, a car is completely unnecessary in San Cristóbal. Public transportation consists of buses, combis (vans) and, of course, taxis. The differences are comfort and price. When Linda and I stay at a house of a friend about an hour's walk out of the center of town, we opt many times for taxis. When I am alone and returning to the house at night, I take a taxi. I enjoy the taxi drivers and the conversations that ensue. From my journal comes the following:

Need information? Want to know the best place for tacos? The quickest way to the Amber Museum? Ask your taxi driver. At about 25 pesos (approximately $2.00) a ride within the city boundaries, a taxi is a real deal. And there are so many of them that your wait is rarely longer than a minute. No, really.

Initiating conversations with your driver is great for practicing Spanish. Many of them have worked in the U.S. and tell harrowing accounts of border crossings. Competition among drivers is fierce

because supply is so high. Some tailgate, some speed, some are preoccupied. My life rests in their hands.

- The Ranter: The rant starts seconds after saying "buenos días"
  and continues at increasing decibels the course of the ride. Rant
  topics include: taxation — especially of the poor and hard-
  working; the crummy daily minimum wage (56 pesos a day
  in San Cristóbal, currently less than $5); the lack of respect
  that the combi drivers have for the taxistas; the streets that
  the government delays repairing; and the 12- to 14-hour work
  schedules.

- The Nice Guy: Smiles, is very polite, low key, drives at a decent
  (read: not overly fast) speed. The one who drove Linda and me
  home yesterday told us about his family of six … three sets of
  twins!

- The Twelve Year Old: OK, he's really 18, so he says, but he
  looks 12. He has rap on the radio and a lead foot. Such has
  been my fear with these young ones that I have lied and told
  them that a recent accident has made me nervous. They don't
  lose face with my story. They don't think I don't trust them, and
  best of all, they slow down.

- The Flirt: I'm over 60 but sometimes light hair compensates for
  wrinkles. I've been asked out a couple of times and have quietly
  demurred.

- The Cell Phone Talker: This fellow spends the entire cab ride
  talking either on the phone or on the dispatch radio. This evening's one-sided conversation went something like this:

Phone rings.

"Hello, my love. Are you still mad?"

"I'm not mad. I just got busy and was preoccupied and didn't call."

"I know you were waiting. Now, don't be una mujercita impudente (an impudent little woman.)"

"Where are you? I can be there is 15 minutes. No, mi cielo, I have a fare right now."

"Wait for me. If you are not there and I get another fare, I'll have to leave."

You get the drift. He hung up as we got out of the cab. After my "hasta luego", I couldn't resist adding "ojalá que todo salga bien con la mujercita." (I hope all goes well with the little woman.)

SICK, SICK, SICK

Traveling and risking getting sick go hand in hand. Airplanes themselves are breeding grounds for illness and several times I have arrived home from a trip to come down with the respiratory ailment from hell two days later. Changing climates, diets and germs or exposing yourself to tropical insects all carry a degree of risk. I asked Jack, an ex-pat who had lived in San Cristóbal for 14 years, if his stomach had toughened up. "Well," he laughed, "About once a year I still get a bout of diarrhea. Guess I got here too late in life for my stomach to completely adapt."

The first time that Bob and I went to Guatemala, I had a pretty good run (no pun intended) of what is referred to as "turista," "the Guates," or "the trots." I was raised in a family in which what happened in the bathroom stayed in the bathroom. It was one of the several issues (along with earnings and sex) relegated to the "unmentionable" realm. No wonder my first marriage was doomed to failure with my in-laws thinking that nothing was funnier than throwing open a bathroom door and snapping a photo of someone on the pot. Thank goodness this didn't happen to me, but I lived in fear that it would.

I had known Bob a year before we set out to spend a month in Guatemala in the summer of 1990. The first couple of weeks of the trip went well, although a few minor bathroom issues cropped up, and I realized that diarrhea was a heated and frequent topic among fellow travelers. In Antigua, after eating in a vegetarian restaurant, my stomach rebelled and knotted up and was determined to purge everything. We were staying in a room that had a curtain between the bedroom and the toilet. A curtain! Noises were not even slightly muted but resounded through the small spaces loud and oh so embarrassingly clear. Every time my stomach cramped and I jumped up and ran behind the curtain, I'd beg Bob to go outside on the patio and wait until I emerged again. Obviously this didn't work well during the night.

By day three, I was weak and raw and tired. I swore that Guatemala and Central America were not for me and I'd never be back. I figured if Bob and I could survive the curtain and the noises and the out-of-sorts whining person into which I had evolved, then maybe our relationship could stand the test of time. I made my way into a doctor's office and it was evident that my tale of woe was just another run-of-the-mill tourist complaint. He loaded me up with healthy flora and soon I was as good as new.

In the past 20 years this has played itself out several times:

- Bob came down with the same ailment just as we were getting on a small plane to fly to Tikal from Guatemala City. There was no toilet on the plane. He held his breath the whole way, relieved beyond words when the plane touched down and a bathroom was once again in reach.

- As a bus waited outside the hotel to take us on a 10-hour ride from Guatemala City to Huehuetenango, close to the Mexican border, I was in the bathroom, head in hands, in despair. How could I get on a bus when I couldn't leave the bathroom? Popping immodium and eating nothing, I boarded. Miraculously I lasted about three hours before nature called, and I persuaded the driver to make a stop for me. This type of travel is not, I repeat, not, fun.

• A case of sciatica flared up while I was leading a group in San Cristóbal and while I was swallowing the number of ibuprophen capsules that my doctor recommended, I didn't realize that I should be taking them with food. So in a few days my stomach was upset. Thinking I had "Montezuma's revenge," I tried the local remedy of Coca-Cola with a lot of lemon juice and bicarbonate of soda. The citrus further aggravated my already acidic stomach and I got worse. Riding in a vehicle made me nauseated and I was dizzy and weak. I somehow managed to lead the group but had to cancel at least one day's excursion. Although I was supposed to continue to northern Guatemala to have a workshop with another non-profit organization, I cancelled and changed my flights so I could go home early. Sick as the proverbial dog, I was accompanied by Linda and Carol. With a doctor's note in hand, Mexicana didn't charge us for the flight change from Tuxtla Gutiérrez to Mexico City. But we still had to re-book the Mexico City-Seattle leg of the trip. Upon arrival at the US Airways counter in Mexico City, agent Jesús took one look at me and compassionately changed our tickets. To this day I say I was saved by Jesús in Mexico City.

• Ecuador, 1999. At the beginning of five weeks in Ecuador, studying and traveling solo, I was making my way from Quito to Cuenca. I made a bit of a detour to the town of Baños to see the picturesque town, the waterfall dedicated to the Virgin and the eco-zoo. Stupidly, oh so stupidly, I ate a salad. I had of course inquired whether it had been washed in purified water and was assured that it had. It wasn't two hours later when the stomach pains hit. I was more annoyed at my own gullibility than I was at the restaurant. And of course, I was scheduled to leave the next morning on the next leg of the journey to Cuenca. Immodium is wonderful, but can't be relied upon 100 percent of the time. Nonetheless, I boarded the bus that would take me to Riobamba. Once there, I found a pharmacist who gave me pills that he promised would cure what ailed me. So as not to tempt fate, I also went on the tried-and-true diet of rice and bananas. The Chinese restaurant in town served me a couple of meals consisting only of white rice. A day later, I was well enough to continue the bus journey south.

- The absolute best story serves as a follow-up to the account of Carol, Martha and me on our adventure trip through Belize, Guatemala and Mexico. Carol, as I mentioned, had a mosquito bite on her head that she'd gotten in Belize. As the trip progressed, it didn't seem to go away, and she continued complaining about it. I admit to being less than compassionate … I thought she was just kvetching. Two weeks after the bite, it was still itching and I was fed up hearing about it. However, I was about to eat a lot of crow. Back in Seattle, now a month after the initial bite, Carol's doctor put her on a course of antibiotics. "You were sweating in the heat and humidity, you scratched the bite, and it got infected," he explained. She dutifully took the pills. Ten days later the pills were gone and the bite site was still itching. Carol made an appointment with the Department of Tropical Medicine at the University of Washington Medical Center. This time the doctor knew what he was looking at.

"Botfly!" he proclaimed. He took a tweezers and, with a little poke, he extracted a larva from Carol's head. Along with being totally grossed out, Carol felt a sense of relief. She hadn't been malingering or making a mountain out of a mosquito bite. Her mosquito had picked up some botfly eggs that had been injected into Carol when she was stung.

Carol was still in a bit of shock when the doctor asked her permission to invite other doctors and interns in to see the larva. He awaited their arrival and then extracted a second botfly larva from her head.

About six months later, I was suffering from an intestinal upset that would just not go away and I finally had made an appointment in the UW Medical Center. While my symptoms were being discussed, I mentioned Carol to the doctor attending me. "Ah," he smiled, "the famous botfly woman! We have preserved those larvae. We don't get the chance to have that experience very often." Carol and her botfly had made a bit of medical history, and I had been impatient with her complaints. This was a lesson learned for me, and Carol and I went on to travel many more times together.

JOURNAL ENTRY APRIL 2011: A VISIT TO THE HUESERO

I'm lying on my stomach, jeans pulled down, blouse off, bra unhooked and the huesero[5] is killing me. His strong hands up and down my spine make me gasp and yelp and lift up off the bed. I'll try anything to alleviate the neck pain I've had the past six months and Ramona

---

[5]   The word "huesero" comes from the Spanish "hueso" which means bone. A huesero deals with the body's structural issues using deep massage. He's like a chiropractor without the adjustments. Sometimes cups are used to pull out the toxins and restore balance, much like the healing art of the Chinese. Skills are honed in apprenticeships and commonly passed down from father to son.

recommended Don Jorge. He's a small, compact man, probably in his late 60s. I have nothing to lose, so he works on me until I am past some of the pain and moving into the kind of pleasure that a deep tissue massage provides.

For some unfathomable reason, "Goldeneye" is playing on the TV next to the bed where I'm lying. It's fairly loud ... maybe to drown out my inadvertent "Ays" and "Ufs."[6] The movie is in English, so I know that Don Jorge does not understand the dialog.

"Ay de mí," I gasp, as Don Jorge digs in.

"Bond, James Bond" says the TV.

"Uf" I moan in protest.

"A martini, shaken, not stirred" intones Sean Connery in his Scottish burr.

"Jesús!"[7] I yell in pain.

And, shortly thereafter there are the sounds of lovemaking emanating from the TV while Don Jorge rips into my vertebra.

Afterwards, I dress and try to cover myself while he turns his back. I notice the pain level is a bit down. "Two more treatments" prescribes Don Jorge. I hand him the one hundred pesos ... about $8.50 U.S.

DECEMBER, 2011: THE DENTIST

Bedside manners of doctors, nurses and dentists in Latin American countries frequently trump bedside manners of medical professionals in the States. I can attest to this. In the

---

6   "Ay" and "Uf" are the Spanish equivalents of "ouch" and "yikes."

7   Jesús, (pron. "hay-soose") is commonly used to express emotion (or pain in this case) and is not considered blasphemous.

early 2000s I landed in the hospital in Cochabamba, Bolivia, with a nasty respiratory infection and severe dehydration. As blood was being taken and an IV inserted, the nurse was stroking my arm, murmuring "Todo bien, preciosa, no te preocupes." (All is well, precious, don't worry.) And now, as I sit in the dentist's chair in San Cristóbal, Dr. Bendaña puts his hand on my shoulder and, in the most sympathetic voice, reassures me with "Oh, Señora, please don't concern yourself. The best thing about teeth is that whatever the problem, it can be resolved. We will take care of you."

About a month earlier, I had a new crown. I had seen my own dentist five times for adjustments, but I still couldn't chew on it without pain and I knew it was still high. I departed for Chiapas still unable to chew on the left side. And my jaw was aching. And as the days evaporated before the group I was to lead arrived, the tooth felt like it moved if I bit on it. I decided to call a dentist whom I had met before and who came highly recommended.

The chain of events may sound straightforward. But let me add that I am a worrier. I obsess, especially at 3 in the morning when I can't get back to sleep as I go over my options. And then go over them again. And again. Do I tough it out and wait two weeks until I return to the States? Do I lead a group when all I can think about is the discomfort in my jaw? Do I take the chance of my jaw swelling up and my needing an emergency root canal and antibiotics in the middle of the itinerary? And soon my stomach is aching and my lower lip is already anticipating the cold sore that will erupt within days from the anxiety. After several increasingly stressful nights, I had resolved to be pro-active and call the dentist.

In Mexico, dentists will actually answer their own phones. In less than an hour, I was in the chair. Dr. Bendaña percussed several teeth and only the newly crowned culprit reacted. "Señora, I am not completely sure, but I think you need a root canal." Relief coursed through my veins as he added, "And my brother is an endodontist." An endondontist! In San Cristóbal!

Within two days I had an appointment and the second Dr. Bendaña, as handsome and reassuring as his brother, completed the endodontic treatment in one 2 ½ hour session. The tooth still needed some time to calm down from the vigorous canal roto-rooting, but the ache in the jaw diminished quickly. Later, back in the States, an endodontist proclaimed the root canal perfect.

I know that you are wondering about the cost. In the States, a root canal on a lower molar can run $1,400 and that doesn't include the restoration required afterward. Luckily my crown emerged intact from the treatment with the exception of the access hole, and Dr. Bendaña placed a filling there. The total was $222. Now I understand the rising popularity of leaving the United States to have heart surgery in India or dentistry in Mexico. Surprisingly, my dental insurance honored that bill. Of course 80 percent of $222 was a lot less than their usual payout. They must have been delighted.

THE INDIGENOUS VIEW OF THE HEALING ARTS

When in San Cristóbal, I highly recommend a visit to the Museo de Medicina Maya. Miguel, the administrator, gives wonderfully informative tours (only in Spanish, unfortunately) to enlighten those visiting from regions that view the practice of medicine from a Western point of view. He explains the difference between "curanderos" (those who heal both physical and emotional difficulties with their knowledge of plants), the hueseros (those who deal with structure and bones), the parteras (the midwives who also deal with menstruation issues) and the shamans (who usually tackle the illnesses of the spirit).

In the indigenous town of San Juan Chamula, a clinic was built and staffed with doctors. However, the townspeople didn't make much use of it. The Western style of medicine was so far afield that the Chamulans couldn't relate, let alone feel comfortable with it. As Mercedes, the guide on my first trip to Chiapas explained, when someone is ill, the patient pays a visit to the local curandero. If the issue is not resolved, a visit to the shaman may be needed. The patient is then engaged in conversation about his family, the town, recent news and is soon feeling comfortable and relaxed. Then the shaman takes the patient's pulse. In this way the source of the illness is determined. It could well be a psychological cause: unresolved anger, a curse, perhaps resentment. The treatment depends on the diagnosis and the next step involves a meeting at the church with the right number of candles, incense, eggs or a chicken, the fermented posh and Coca-Cola. Patients were comfortable with such treatments.

At the Western-modeled clinic, the physicians didn't begin with comforting small talk. They didn't know the family of the patient. They began with symptoms and many times it was a particular symptom that was treated rather than viewing the body as a whole. Indigenous men prohibited their wives from seeing or being touched by male doctors. Cultures clashed.

Disrespect of indigenous women by doctors includes women who delivered babies in a hospital and returned home ignorant of the fact that their tubes had been tied. Other women had birth control devices implanted without permission. They would find out later when complications developed. Add this to the lack of education about how the human body functions, and results can be disastrous.

When I first met Flavia in 2003, she was unwell. Female problems, Ramona told me. She was going in for surgery and she was quite scared about it. When I talked with her later, she wasn't sure what had been done. Years later she had a hysterectomy and I visited her house just three weeks after the surgery. I shared with her the fact that it took six weeks after my own surgery to feel really well again. She seemed surprised and then hopeful. I got the idea that no one had told her what to expect.

About two years ago, a hospital for the indigenous was opened with much fanfare in San Cristóbal. As a state-funded project, Chiapas could point to the hospital as a real feather in its cap, and it was highly publicized. At about the same time, two of our scholarship girls expressed a desire to become nurses. Linda and I were delighted with this aspiration and encouraged by the new hospital. Then the bomb dropped. The new hospital didn't hire indigenous nurses. And the indigenous patients were victims of condescension, rudeness and impatience. More racism. More evidence that education plays a key role. But Mujeres de Maiz Opportunity Foundation only works on part of that equation as we focus on providing access to education for indigenous women and children. The non-indigenous population needs that education, too. They need to learn respect for the indigenous and the traditional ways.

Couldn't the Maya and Western systems of medicine be somehow melded together? If the knowledge of medicinal plants were integrated with western drugs; if the personal approach of the shaman could be insinuated into the colder, professional approach of the physicians; if the ways of the midwife were blended with a hospital birth, wouldn't everyone benefit?

MEXICAN TIME

I sit waiting for Ramona. She set the time, she decided the place. I have known Ramona for almost eight years now. I am the picture of patience although she is 30 minutes late. She is *always* late. If she appears only 15 minutes late, I consider her on time. The longest she has kept me waiting is 45 minutes past our appointed time. I am wondering if she is going to set a new record. Only once has she not shown up … it was early and she overslept … anyone can do that. I have learned to bring something to read or I write to pass the time.

She arrives, 35 minutes late, all smiles. Mexican time requires no excuses. I am glad to see her, as always.

For those of you familiar with Mexico, I don't have to tell you that two concepts of time south of our border are as alien to those of us north of the border as driving on the left-hand side of the road. The first is punctuality. We are so used to time being an immovable force, one that drives us like a whip. Arriving late is not acceptable, time is money, don't waste time.

Consider the following scenario:

You are seated in the office of Sr. Martínez in Mexico. You have a 1:30 appointment. You are there precisely at 1:25. At 1:40

you check your watch. At 1:45 you wonder: Did *I* get the time right? Did *el señor* get the time right?

1:50: Could there have been an accident??

2:00: Did I get the *day* right?

2:05: I do have other things I could be doing. (tapping my foot)

2:10: Where the hell is he? (angry now, gritting teeth)

2:15: How *&#%# rude, keeping me waiting like this!

And at 2:20 the door opens, and Sr. Martínez enters with a warm, genuine smile and a handshake. Your annoyance dissolves as the meeting begins.

So where had the "late" Sr. Martínez been? You'll probably never know, but chances are he was with friends or family, both of which are much more important than keeping an eye on the clock. The rigidity of time as we know it doesn't exist: Time is stretchable. Time is for our use, not the other way around. Time is a loose construct.

"Uno no es un tren" (One is not a train) is the title of a short story that I used to teach in my Spanish classes. The above frustration is illustrated in a bit of a different way. A person trying to set a time to meet a friend was unable to get the friend to be minute-specific and finally lost all patience. Paraphrasing, "Place is specific. You don't agree to meet someone at a specific location and have them show up a block away. Time is also specific, that's what it's for."

What I call "mañanitis" is the second concept that defies typical practice in the United States. Ex-pats learn early that this "infirmity" is totally ingrained in the Latin American character and bucking it causes grey hair at best and heart attacks at worst. A woman I knew had relocated to Antigua, Guatemala, a lovely city in the highlands. Her washing machine had broken and the repairman said he'd be out to fix it "mañana." She stayed home all day and he didn't show up, so with slight annoyance she called him again. "Mañana, Señora, vengo." Reassured that he would indeed come the following day, she stayed home the second day but still no repairman. She called a third time, more than mildly vexed, and with no excuses he told her not to worry, tomorrow. It took several days before he showed up and fixed the machine. Life gets in the way of time and work.

I take small groups to Chiapas. I have to set times for meetings, for excursions, for transportation to the airport. And amazingly, these are all respected within minutes. But in everyday life, hey, we Americans are a bit uptight, a bit anal. We don't enjoy the minute. Instead, we are controlled by it. And as many times as I've visited Mexico, I still find myself talking myself through the impatience. I am convinced, however, that the relaxed attitude toward time is a healthier and much less stressful way to live.

NOISE

When I arrived in San Cristóbal with the first group back in 2005, we were all exhausted after the full day of travel. We grabbed some dinner and settled into our rooms at NaBolom, a center for the study and photography of the Lacandon Indians as well as a hotel. At the time it was reasonably priced and the rooms and gardens were lovely. In short, it was a tranquil respite after a long day of airports, airplanes and buses. But, first time tour leader that I was, I neglected to mention the firecrackers. So, the first thing the next morning, a member of my group said she was a bit disturbed hearing what she thought was gunfire at dawn.

The Mexicans love firecrackers and use any opportunity to set them off. Birthdays, festivals, weddings, you name it, are just not complete without the jarring bangs and rushing wind that accompany the exploding fireworks. I never figured out the reason for them to be exploded quite so early, but "así es" (that's just the way it is). The number of daily "bangs" increases exponentially on important religious holidays or citywide celebrations.

Sergio Castro (check out the documentary "El Andalón" that showcases this fascinating individual) has another take on the firecracker phenomenon. Trained as a veterinarian, years ago he realized the devastating effect of firecrackers on many indigenous men who set them off ... namely, burns. Sergio learned to treat burns and for years has made burn care his specialty. He accepts no money but does request donations and medical supplies that he uses in treatment. When I hear the ear-splitting "cohetes," I think of Sergio.

If the firecrackers don't wake you, the roosters will. Or the trucks with the loudspeakers endlessly playing "Raindrops Keep Falling on Your Head" interspersed with a commercial for buying bottled water. Over and over. Or the trucks selling propane, which drag an assortment of metal on the ground behind them that simultaneously announces their imminent arrival as well as permanently sets your teeth on edge and damages your hearing.

And while on the subject of noise, Americans[8] are considered noisy tourists. On buses, in restaurants, not only are American voices overly loud, but Americans raise their voices in the streets, usually to yell at their friends who have moved a bit out of earshot. This is definitely not considered cool. It's an interesting contradiction that a much noisier culture on the whole disapproves of loud voices.

---

[8]   The word "American" refers to people from the United States. However, the use of the word "americano" in Spanish can be a sensitive issue as all people in this hemisphere are, literally, "americanos." Even using the phrase "norteamericanos" includes Canadians and Mexicans. As I have found that some Latin Americans feel that people from the U.S. have usurped the word "americanos" when speaking Spanish, I use the word "estadounidenses" (United States-ians) instead. Unfortunately, there is no direct translation.

TRES FIESTAS

LA GUADALUPANA

First you notice the runners carrying torches on the roads. Then you notice that many of them run barefoot. Behind each runner, a truck slowly follows. It is decorated with palm branches and filled with people wearing tee-shirts adorned with pictures of La Virgen de Guadalupe. As the December 12 date approaches, runners and trucks increase, slowing traffic everywhere to a crawl. The torchbearers run in relays, switching runners every kilometer or so. They are members of churches or local religious organizations. They have trained for months and have offered up their devotion to La Virgen.

Certain cities have churches dedicated to her that are particularly revered. Tlaxcala is one, as is Mexico City. And so is San Cristóbal de las Casas. La Iglesia de La Virgen sits on a hill to the east side of the city center. It crowns the east-west andador (the walking street) and attracts city dwellers and tourists alike. The church, at the top of a series of steps, is somehow very welcoming. While not as large as, for example, Santo Domingo or La Merced, it's very pretty and airy, with an outside garden dedicated to the Virgin.

Patricia, a former scholarship recipient, ran with a group that first drove to Mexico City and then ran back to San Cristóbal, a distance of about 650 miles. Others run in from more local communities. For the entire week before the 12ᵗʰ, the runners come in. They run through the city, down the walking street and up the steps to the church. They chant, they cheer, they carry banners and statues and their facial expressions express the joy at the end of the run, their mission completed, their promise fulfilled. As the week goes on, more and more groups arrive until during the last two days it's almost a constant stream of runners.

In 1531, in the desert near Mexico City, a peasant named Juan Diego saw an apparition who told him she was the Virgin Mother and that she wanted a church built right on that spot. When the bishop scoffed at the man's tale, the Virgin appeared again (on December 12) and gave Juan roses as proof to show the bishop. When Juan Diego opened his cloak full of roses, an image of Mary was found on his cloak. Needless to say, the church was built on the site requested, a site that turned out to be where an Aztec temple had stood and had been destroyed.

December 8 is considered the date of the immaculate conception of the Virgin Mary. She, too, was conceived without sin. So this week is particularly noteworthy in predominantly Catholic Mexico. About two days before the 12ᵗʰ, the walking street fills with pint-sized Juan Diegos and Virgins making their way down the walking street and up the steps to the church to be blessed. The boys, from infants to maybe 10 years old, all wear rustic rebozos and have penciled-in mustaches. The girls are more varied in appearance, but most have lovely long dresses and some have halos.

The barrio (neighborhood) of the church hangs plasticized papel picado (paper cut-outs) of the Virgin across the walking street for several blocks before the church. The carnival appears a few days in advance and the vendors set up stalls on the sidewalks selling food, toys, and images of the Virgin on tee shirts, candles and bandanas. Traffic is restricted. The church itself

La Iglesia de La Virgen de Guadalupe, San Cristóbal de Las Casas
Photo by Judith Pasco

starts to fill up with thousands of bouquets of flowers left by the devotees. Inside the church, there's a brightly-lit life-sized depiction of Juan Diego and La Virgen. The picture of the Virgin behind the altar is bordered by neon lights of various colors, which blink off and on. On December 12th, the blocks closest to the church are packed. I make my way through the crowd, wearing my new tee-shirt with a sparkly Virgen de Guadalupe on the front. I wear it in solidarity and in respect.

There is something ... a mystery, a force ... that is compelling. Her compassion and suffering spill out of the images and there's an energy that feels almost tangible. I decide to climb the steps, weaving my way around families and groups of friends, stopping two or three times to catch my breath. The church is overflowing with people and flowers. A Mass is in session. I stand on tiptoes to see in the doors and the palpable love and devotion of the faithful is overwhelming. Something is at work here, and I envy it. Tears spring to my eyes, and I whisper "thank you, thank you."

ZAPATISTA NEW YEAR'S
JANUARY 1, 2009

When Linda and I got back from our errands, my husband Bob looked like the proverbial cat that had swallowed the canary.

"I met someone today, and this'll interest you," he began, "you know how we have heard about the big New Year's celebration out in Oventic?"

As I nodded, he continued, "Well, I was out in the street in front of the house and I saw a gringa loading up her truck. I don't know why, but I went over to say hello to her. Turns out she has some connections with the Zapatistas and was just then heading out to Oventic to spend three days at the celebration. When I told her we'd be interested in going, she said we should just show up and see how it goes."

My brain was off and running. Oventic! Zapatistas! How could we not go?

Oventic is an important Zapatista community. In 1997, when Carol and I traveled to Chiapas as unofficial election observers, we were part of a group that had driven to Oventic and tried to get in. But it's a fenced community and no one there at the time had the authority to admit a van of strangers. Chiapas was a bit more tense then, as it was only three years after the Zapatista uprising and the elections currently in progress were rather heated. We had seen roadblocks to prevent people from entering communities to vote; we had seen ballot boxes set on fire; we had passed through a large group of stern-looking men, all carrying machetes.

But this was January 1, 2009. The Zapatistas, still a force to be reckoned with, had largely retired from public confrontation and were fighting their battles quietly in their own way. I admire the Zapatistas. They have raised consciousness and brought a sense of dignity to indigenous people. The autonomous Zapatista communities do not recognize the authority of the Mexican government because the indigenous population has been ignored, disparaged, discriminated against and harassed for centuries. The Zapatista villages prohibit alcohol, arms and drugs. Women share equal status with men. Let me be clear: Mujeres is an organization that is in no way political. But personally, I believe that the Zapatistas set the stage for the indigenous movement toward equality and I respect people who live their vision.

Linda, her husband Tim, Bob and I woke early on New Year's Day. We found a taxi that would take us to Oventic, about an hour away over curvy mountain roads. We knew that this was a special celebration that had started a couple of days earlier and would continue for several more. The Zapatistas were celebrating the 15th anniversary since the rebellion and the 25th year since they first identified themselves as a movement.

For a quarter mile in both directions from the entrance of Oventic, the shoulders of the road were filled with parked cars, buses and trucks. Our driver let us off at the entrance, and we could see a lot of people on the other side of the fence. The gate, however, was locked.

We stood there for a few minutes until a man with the typical Zapatista ski mask approached.

"Good morning and Happy New Year," I began, "May we come in?"

"I need all your passports," he responded. I handed mine over and the others also complied, but I could see a hint of indecision in Tim's eyes before his passport was passed over.

"Wait here," the masked greeter instructed and left.

Not more than five minutes later he reappeared, opened the gate, and ushered us into the Oficina de Vigilencia (the Vigilence Office), now in service as a place to "vet" the visitors. There, three men sat at a long table, all wearing the ski masks. The man in the middle was painstakingly copying information from our passports onto a large ledger. We stood there until he finished.

"Why are you here?" was the first question put to us.

"Well," I said, "We heard it was your 25th anniversary and we wanted to celebrate with you."

"How long are you staying?"

"We can only stay a few hours."

And that was it. Our passports were returned and we exited the building and started down the road toward where the festival was being held. The road was lined with vendors selling CDs, jewelry, posters, and so on. I felt an excitement in the air, an energy, and I could see that Linda felt it, too.

At the bottom of the road was a stage and the area around it was jammed with people. As we looked down the incline, Linda was struggling to catch her breath as the reality of where we were hit her. Mist was rising up from the bottom of the hill like steam from hot broth. On both sides of the stage were tents, so close together as to make walking really difficult, and people were everywhere, sleeping, talking and eating. There were a huge number of celebrants in front of the stage itself. Stopping there, I had time to look around and marvel at the variety of individuals that made up the crowd.

There were many, both men and women, wearing Zapatista masks or the trademark bandana over their nose and mouth. There were people in indigenous dress from many Chiapas communities as well as from other parts of Mexico. Because communities wear clothing that is readily identifiable, we could see that many different villages were represented. And there were many foreigners, some from Europe, some from Canada and the United States, all mingling together and celebrating the Zapatista anniversary and the start of another year.

The performances on the stage were colorful and varied. Singers, dancers and poets were wildly enthusiastic. An artist with a red bandana covering his face was painting a huge picture of the Virgin of Guadalupe on the ground. "This is Zapatista Woodstock," said Linda, looking rather rapturous. I looked around and almost pinched myself and when I looked at Linda, we both had tears in our eyes. "What a privilege to be present at this occasion," I thought in amazement, shaking my head in wonderment at how fortunate I was.

We were dying to take photos. We were also unsure of the etiquette of such an occasion and didn't want to offend anyone. Finally, Linda spotted a young man taking pictures. We watched him a bit and nobody said anything to him. So we went ahead and tried to capture a bit of the magic of the experience on film.

When we pulled ourselves away from the stage, we walked around the community, teeming with visitors. Most of the buildings had murals on their exteriors, including the school.

The mountain mist moved in and out making the whole scene a bit surreal. Linda and I made our way to the long line of latrines that were, on this, the third day of the fest, overflowing. I didn't envy the folks who were staying for the complete celebration. The toilet situation certainly was not going to get any better. I could see a few people pulling up the stakes of their tents and I wondered if this was their planned leaving date or if the latrine situation had precipitated their departure.

After a couple of hours we figured we had better try to arrange our ride back to San Cristóbal. We walked back up the road, through the locked gate and onto the road. No taxis were in evidence.

"I see a couple of trucks," noted Bob, and we all looked. People were standing in the back and holding on to slotted wooden sides. I strongly doubted that I could stand in the back of a truck for an hour … especially considering that these roads are some of the curviest roads I'd ever traveled on. We all nixed the idea. A few minutes later, a van appeared and we saw people only in the front seats. It was going slowly, negotiating the tight road with all the parked cars. I motioned to the driver, leaned in and politely asked for a ride and he consented. We had a great conversation all the way back, about his family and how he'd been celebrating the New Year. When we mentioned that we'd been at Oventic, the talk became more constrained and we got the impression that they did not approve of the Zapatista movement. The baby in the front seat with the mom looked well-fed, well-clothed and happy. Hmm, I mused, isn't that what the Zapatistas want for their own children? Our driver dropped us off on the outskirts of San Cristóbal, we thanked him profusely, as he refused any compensation, and we grabbed a taxi to downtown.

That night, playing "Outburst" with Bob, Linda and Tim and eating leftover sopa de pan in our rented house, I kept thinking about the day and the celebration. I thought how such celebrations must be so needed, so anticipated, after years of struggle, years of harassment, years of deprivation. Overflowing latrines would not stop the party, nor put a damper on the high spirits. And yet, the people who live in Oventic know that when the party is over and the community is cleaned up, life must go on. The struggle is far from over, but they will continue living it, with renewed hope and the feeling of solidarity that so many people from so many places left with them. As I fell asleep, I kept seeing one of the banners displayed over the stage.

> *2009 2009 2009 2009 2009 2009*
> *OTRO AÑO EN RESISTENCIA*

LA FIESTA DE SAN LORENZO: AUGUST, 2011

San Lorenzo is the patron saint of Zinacantán. During the second week of August, in the town's biggest festival, he is honored by ceremonies, dances, flowers in the church, and bareback horse races through the streets. Women weave for months in advance, as this festival is the showcase for their wearable art.

Linda and I were invited to the house of Iliana and Josefa (two of our first scholarship recipients) to celebrate the festival. Just before the horse races started, their mother, Rigoberta, appeared with beautiful shawls in the latest colors and draped them over our shoulders. She wanted us to enjoy the experience dressed like Zinacantecas. I smiled to myself because a couple of tall gringas (relatively so) stood out even more when sporting the colorful shawls. Never do I feel so drab as when I am in

Zinacantán, usually attired in my dull (maybe even throwaway) travel clothes of practical khaki, tan and denim.

Suitably attired, we followed la abuelita (the grandmother) down the streets to the plaza. The religious officials in black and blue robes with gold trim reminiscent of King Henry VIII's court were chanting in front of the church prior to entering and dancing in the flower-bedecked side chapel. A band played in the gazebo and several men were passed out on the ground. Spirited horses at the end of the street waited for the signal that the races would begin. Men wearing straw hats, with hundreds of multi-colored, waist-length ribbons that cascaded down their backs, sat astride the horses sharing bottles of posh prior to the breakneck ride down the street. We noticed that several men were putting the bottle to their lips but were not imbibing. A wise move, in my humble and non-Zinacanteca opinion.

A procession of community officials in long black woolen robes and red turbans filed by and a huge bandshell was being erected to house the several bands that were on the docket that evening. Dancing would continue well into the night. But it was the incredible weaving and embroidery that dazzled us. Every indigenous community in the highlands of Chiapas has a tradition of weaving that has evolved for centuries. According to Chip Morris, author of <u>Living Maya</u> and perhaps the foremost expert on Maya textile history, design and trends in this region, the fashion in the indigenous communities changes much more quickly than it used to, due to increased exposure to global trends via the internet and other media. And the Festival of San Lorenzo in Zinacantán displays the colors, style and changes in a riot of shawls and cortes (traditional wrap around woven skirts) that dazzle the eyes. The women of this town design the new patterns and use daring color combinations in the clothes they weave, embroider, cross-stitch, and yes, even paint, for the year's biggest festival. Gorgeous gaggles of women move

Horse racers in the festival of San Lorenzo, Zinacantán
Photo by Judith Pasco

through the streets and across the plaza that sits in front of the church in a kaleidoscope of brilliant, sparkly attire covered with arrays of embroidered flowers. The color! La fiesta provides an opportunity to display their creativity and simultaneously admire the designs of others. The entire town becomes a catwalk in the fashion show of the year.

MARIELENA AND THE MUDDY SHOE

Running an organization such as *Mujeres* does not involve working solely with the women of the cooperative. Over the years I've come to feel at home in San Cristóbal. The American ex-pat community is small and includes warm, friendly people. Ann and John are building a boutique hotel. Bela is a longtime inhabitant, running a B and B with a lovely garden. Jack, whose son lives in my town in Washington State, and his wife are active on the photography scene. Margaret manages the band Sak Tzevul, whose original sound is based on traditional music from Zinacantán. With permission, one of their tracks serves as background music for the Mujeres de Maiz Opportunity Foundation's video.

Roberto, with whom I've had a business relationship since 2005, has become my friend. He and his family offer airport pickup service and excursions. Since I met Roberto (and his brothers, father and uncle), he almost died in a terrible accident, got married and became a father to a curly-haired little girl who looks just like him. He generously offers me the use of a house he owns when I am in town.

And then there's MariElena. Every year in December, I lead an 11-day tour in Chiapas. The group is small … usually between five and eight participants. For the past three years, I have arranged accommodations at a small family run hotel that I've come to like very much. Booking several rooms for 11 nights is a respectable reservation, and the owner, MariElena, her niece, Carita, and the maid, Mercedes, and I have become comfortable with each other.

In December 2010 and April 2011, I complained to MariElena of my painful neck, which had been diagnosed with arthritis and degenerative disc disease. In April she suggested that I see a well-know healer but lamented that he was out of the country. "When you come back in August," she promised, "I will take you to see him. You know, Don Gilberto takes his healing skills all over the world. My husband, who is a physician, avails himself of Don Gilberto's services."

When Linda and I returned to San Cristóbal in the first part of August, I brought with me a wooden animal puzzle. It was a duplicate of a puzzle I had with me on my previous trip, which I gave to the daughter of Roberto. MariElena had seen it in my room and had asked if I could get another one for her new grandchild.

We stopped by the hotel to deliver the puzzle. Despite exhaustive conventional therapies, my neck was still bothering me and I wanted to see Don Gilberto. Linda heard MariElena mention a trip to the mountains and the concern on her face — how many hours was the trip, what should we anticipate — was alleviated when the hotel matron explained that the healer's house was only a short distance away off a main road.

We set out in MariElena's car through the city and started up a muddy, gravel road that did indeed appear as if it would go up and up into the mountains. Within a quarter of a mile, the road deteriorated. Summer is the rainy season and the strong flowing gullies of water washing down from the mountains had made the road look like a topographical map of hills and canyons.

"We'll walk," both Linda and I pleaded, horrified both at the state of the road and MariElena's stalwart determination to drive it. Her car was not equipped for this and soon the loose stones were flying and her wheels spinning and she could go no farther.

We all agreed that she should back down the hundred yards or so to where she could park and we could continue on foot. In a matter of seconds, however, the rear right wheel went over a deep gouge and the car bottomed out with a heart- wrenching CLUNK. My stomach sank. I opened the door and saw that the level of the road on my side was even with the running boards. My hopes went further into the toilet when I got out of the car and saw that the back wheel was hanging over the deep gully and the chassis was sitting on the dirt. Linda climbed out of the back seat and the two of us exchanged horrified looks.

Just then a young man came down the road — "road" at this point being a total euphemism — in a small jeep-like vehicle, exactly what was needed to manage this terrain.

"¿Nos puede ayudar?" I asked him, and with the good grace I have come to expect of the people here, he answered, "Con todo gusto." (with much pleasure.)

He was a young man, rather tall, and his bare arms evidenced some rather well-developed muscles. He took one look at the back wheel, told MariElena to accelerate, and he LIFTED the car out of the hole and pushed until the wheel was on even ground again.

I was speechless. When he first leaned over, I feared the car would roll backward onto him. I hadn't realized that I had been literally holding my breath. He offered to do the necessary backing up for MariElena, but she demurred. He directed her until she managed to get down the hill far enough to where the road damage was minimal. We all thanked him profusely, and he was gone.

Don Gilberto lives about 500 yards up the sad excuse for a road. The shoes that MariElena was wearing were black pumps with an inch heel. Linda had tennis shoes, and I sported my trusty Keen's. The mud in the road was more like a slick clay and the uneven surface and loose rocks were not intended for smooth-soled pumps. It was also obvious that MariElena had not been challenging herself aerobically. Along with gingerly watching her footing, she was huffing and puffing and her forehead was covered with a sheen of sweat. Linda's concerns about the mountains and the road were replaced with the worry of MariElena's possible imminent demise.

Don Gilberto's house sat around the corner, and MariElena gamely started up the slick stepping stones that led to his porch, gaily calling out to the healer, announcing our arrival. I was directly behind her and Linda followed. A shout from MariElena stopped us short. "¡Mi zapato!" she cried.

I was too close to see, but Linda realized that the mud had claimed MariElena's shoe and she was balancing on one foot, trying not to put the bare foot down. While I supported the single-shoed woman, Linda moved around and extracted the shoe from the mud and placed it within reach of her bare foot. By now we were all doubled over laughing hysterically.

We recovered enough to negotiate the remainder of the muddy walkway where Don Gilberto was waiting for us. He took me in immediately to a large room with an altar made up of flower arrangements, candles and religious figures from Jesus to

Buddha. I sat with my back to him on a tiny stool, still hearing MariElena's laughter outside the door. He sprayed my neck with something cold. Linda watched and told me that he made his hands into almost claws as he worked his way up my back and into my neck and shoulders. I gasped a few times from the pain, and the treatment was over in 10 minutes. Arrangements were made for a return visit the following day.

All the way back, MariElena, Linda and I laughed. We laughed about the road, the car, and her muddy shoe, which she said she had feared would be sucked down into the mud and never seen again. Although Don Gilberto's treatment had virtually no effect on my aching neck, the experience as a whole became an enjoyable memory. MariElena and I can't see each other without making "shoe" references. Shared stories make for closer relationships and MariElena and I had just moved into the next phase of friendship.

It is imperative to have a support system, as I painfully learned during my visit to Chiapas in 2003 when I fled after only two weeks. The indigenous women with whom we partner, the ex-pats, the business relationships that slowly evolve into friendships, all deepen the level of involvement and the strength of attachment. All combined make up the love that I feel strongly when I am there and that keeps pulling me back when I'm away.

PART IV

GROWTH AND EVOLUTION: A FOUNDATION TAKES SHAPE

MUJERES DE MAIZ BIRTH: 2006

Bob and I stood in the torrential rain and watched the streets fill and spill water over the tops of the high curbs. Cars were up to their hubcaps in water, and the streets that had been full of people minutes before were deserted except for one intrepid young man sloshing his way along oblivious of his clothing plastered to his body and his soaked shoes. I had been in San Cristóbal three times before during July and August and, although it is the rainy season, I had never seen this much rain.

This was my first trip in an official capacity. *Mujeres de Maiz Opportunity Foundation* had come into being in the autumn of 2005. In a meeting with six of the travelers from the summer trip, a decision was made to find a way to support education for the women and girls of the cooperative. Iliana was the impetus: a scholarship to study English. Five of the six board members were teachers. All six of us fervently believe that education was a hugely important piece lacking in the lives of the women. Education opens doors, provides opportunities and reduces class differences. Our focus would be education in any form.

We had named ourselves after the cooperative, Mujeres de Maíz En Resistencia. "En Resistencia" has to do with the women refusing to buy in to government or world organizations that try to dictate terms to third-world countries. The women wanted self-sustainability on their terms, not on DuPont's, Monsanto's or the World Bank's. The women also are in resistance to old mores, to men having the final say, to indigenous people being disrespected.

Our name had been chosen with care. Although we were going to be the education niche of the cooperative, we didn't want to limit the concept of education just to scholarships. Using the word "opportunity" opened up possibilities. The pronunciation of our name has caused some difficulties. Maybe in retrospect we should have just called it "Women of Corn Opportunity Foundation," because a number of people use the English translation when referring to us. I've had to sound out the "mujeres" to "moo-hair-aise" and the "maíz" to "mah-eese" countless times.

Mujeres de Maiz (maíz is accented in Spanish but not on our organization name) refers to the Maya creation myth from the Popul Vuh. The creator, Heart of the Sky, wanted to populate the earth with beings that would remember where they came from and be respectful. After creating animals, he realized that they could not speak his name. So he created man out of mud, but the experiment was less than successful as mud beings were lopsided and couldn't turn their heads. The second attempt resulted in the creation of wooden people, but they were inflexible and empty. Heart of the Sky, frustrated, crushed them and they became monkeys. The third attempt utilized corn and cornmeal, and the resultant beings had flesh and blood and a heart with feeling. Not only were people created from corn, but corn is the single-most important food in Maya culture. Corn tortillas are made daily from the ground corn, and no Maya house is complete without its "milpa" or corn patch by the dwelling. Corn, grown and eaten with beans and squash, forms a nutritionally complete diet. Our name, *"Mujeres de Maiz,"* is packed to the brim with meaning and history.

Linda, the treasurer, and I painstakingly filled out the forms for our 501(c) (3) status in January 2006. Midsummer arrived and we were still awaiting the IRS ruling. We had been advised that after 9/11 new organizations were carefully vetted. Homeland Security needed to verify that we weren't smuggling arms or supporting terrorist activities. In August, we received word that we had two tasks to complete prior to our approval. Not surprisingly, we were given only two weeks to accomplish the tasks AND have the documents back in the hands of the IRS. If not, we were assured that our application would be thrown out and have to be re-filed.

One of the tasks was not difficult, as it was to include certain verbiage in our bylaws. We complied. But the second task involved a document that we needed to obtain from the State of Washington. With the given time frame of two weeks in mind, I placed a call to the appropriate state office. I was told that the document would be in our hands in six weeks. But could we come in person? I queried. Linda, always ready for a road trip, practically jumped in her car for the three-hour drive to Olympia. Once there, obtaining the needed document took her all of 10 minutes. We overnighted the materials to the IRS, and they arrived well before their rather arbitrary and unreasonable deadline.

So this visit to San Cristóbal was official. We were funding Iliana's scholarship and giving a small stipend to Ramona. I carried the money, not much really, in my waist belt. Ramona and I met at the bank and set up a dedicated account to *Mujeres de Maiz OF*. I need to interject a few words about Ramona. In addition to serving as the coordinator for the cooperative, she agreed to work with us as well. She is an amazing woman who devotes her life to indigenous women. Because she is not indigenous, and thus can be seen as objective when dealing with the women in the cooperative that hail from as many as 12 communities, she has earned their trust and respect. I have watched her handle difficult situations with aplomb. She has a great sense of humor. Along with the officers in the cooperative, she helps organize the agendas for the bi-monthly workshops. Ramona is the reason that *Mujeres de Maiz OF* operates so smoothly. I am honored to call her my friend.

The rain continued daily. In the mornings, the sky would be cloudless and an intense blue. By noon, the clouds would start rolling in and by 1 or 2 in the afternoon, the rain was torrential. Usually it lasted fewer than a couple of hours but it definitely was an obstacle to be dealt with. According to the guidebooks, the rainy season lasts from June to October. I have been in San Cristobal at the end of July, first of August, and encountered little rain, or rain predominantly during the night. During this trip we experienced the rain every single day.

Bob and I had been invited out to the home of Iliana's mother and sisters. They live in the municipality of Zinacantán, about 20 minutes by combi outside of San Cristóbal. Of all the communities that belong to the cooperative, Zinacantán is the nearest. It is still a bit of a mountain drive, which affords a view of the hundreds of greenhouses where flowers are grown as a commercial crop. Before leaving San Cristóbal, Ramona led us through the main market where we purchased tunas (cactus) and bananas for a gift. I learned that one never arrives anywhere without a gift.

The combi pulled up by the church and Ramona, Bob and I walked uphill about half a mile to Iliana's house. The household consisted of her mother, her three sisters and her grandmother. Iliana's mother, Rigoberta, was married young and went to live in the home of her in-laws, as is the tradition. She was a hard worker and birthed four daughters in 13 years. Her husband was an alcoholic, an all-too-familiar scenario. Not only do indigenous men have a propensity toward alcoholism, but also from an early age the religious ceremonies in which they participate require the imbibing of posh, a rot-gut sugar-cane or corn-based liquor.

Most festivals include the sad sight of a good number of men passed out on the sidewalk or in front of the churches. Hand-in-hand with the alcoholism comes domestic violence, and Rigoberta was no stranger to that. When her husband died in his early 30s from drink, I would hazard a guess that Rigoberta breathed a sigh of relief.

With the death of their son, Rigoberta's in-laws threw her and her daughters out, and they returned to live with her mother in a very small, humble house. Undaunted and ambitious, Rigoberta weaved. She had four young girls to raise. She sold her weavings until she could ask for a loan to build a bigger house. She built a home with a main room and two small adjacent sleeping rooms. It had a concrete floor. She paid back the loan and continued to look for ways to better the living situation of the family. She grew flowers on a plot of her late husband's land. The oldest daughter, Josefa, contributed to the weavings and also worked in San Cristóbal. Her earnings helped support the family. The youngest, Carlita, was still in primary school.

Rigoberta greeted us effusively. Ramona told me that when she first met Rigoberta, she only spoke Tsotsil. Now, just a few years later, she spoke a functional Spanish. The kitchen was a separate building with a dirt floor and the traditional tortilla-making comal. Chickens and painfully skinny cats wound around our feet. The fruit from the peach trees added to the household income. The grandmother spoke no Spanish but smiled a welcoming toothless grin before leaving to herd her sheep to the hills to graze. Fourteen lambs were born this year, and a stray dog killed eight of them.

Iliana, daughter number three, the recipient of our first scholarship, had the most drive, according to Rigoberta. "She does everything without being asked. She weaves, she cleans, she cooks, she studies, and she never complains."

This was mainly a getting-acquainted visit. Soon, Iliana arrived home from her classes. Her eyes flashed with enthusiasm when she spoke about starting the preliminary classes in a few months that will pave the path to the university. "I'll work hard," she promised. She smiled shyly and looked down at the ground. I was impressed by the family and their work ethic in the face of so many obstacles. Rigoberta pressed a shawl and a scarf into my hands, and Carlita gave Bob a sack of hard peaches.

On Saturday I attended the women's bi-monthly reunion in my official capacity for the first time. I told the women a bit about our intentions with *Mujeres de Maiz Opportunity Foundation* and how we wanted to help them with access to education. Molly, one of our board members, had given me 20 pairs of good cutting scissors to carry to the women, and I had gathered some children's books in Spanish. I presented the scholarship to Iliana and with it a Spanish-English dictionary. Books are incredibly expensive in Mexico, and a good dictionary for a language major is a must. The women were attentive but not overly enthusiastic. I chalked it up to a very natural lack of trust in our commitment. Gringas come and gringas go. Promises are made and not kept or kept for a short period of time and then forgotten. The resolve in me strengthened. Silently, I gave my word to them and to me.

CRITICISMS/QUESTIONS FROM OUR SUPPORTERS

"Your name is too god-damned long." (This note came with a check after our first fund-raising letter.)

Well, yes, it is.

"Why don't you help people in your own country?"

A couple of reasons. First, I believe that boundaries on maps are artificial means of categorizing peoples and terrain. Just look at how the map of Africa has changed in the past 20 years, or how the European countries were carved up and changed after World War I and II. Texas used to belong to Mexico. Chiapas used to belong to Guatemala. People are people, period, which brings me to my second reason. You work where you are called to work. Some people see "calling" as a religious term. Maybe it is. I was "pulled" to Chiapas. Nothing in my English heritage set me up to be a "Maya-phile," but there it is. I am support-ing education where education needs to be supported. As an organization, we support women where women are discounted and devalued. I admire people who have a cause, wherever and whatever that cause may be.

"Why can't you support our own indigenous communities?"

See above response.

"Don't you think women are empowered enough?" (Asked by a middle-aged white male who had seen my "Empowering Women" license plate frame)

Oh, for heaven's sake. Come to Chiapas and walk in the women's shoes.

"Can't you just be 'Women of Corn?' 'Mujeres de Maiz' is too hard to pronounce."

We took our name from the cooperative. Many times before I speak, I am introduced as being from the Women of Corn Opportunity Foundation. That's fine, as long as they donate to us. OK, that's a joke. Or is it?

SNAPSHOTS FROM DECEMBER 2008

Snapshot number one:

Covered with dust from riding in the back of a pickup truck at a bat-out-of-hell speed up a mountain "bus plunge" road, Linda, Tim, Bob and I were now walking the rest of the way up to the community high above the city of Yajalón. We carried pineapples, tangerines and beans in our packs to give as gifts. We were surrounded by paradise: coffee plantations, high mountains, views as far as one could see: green, green, green. Happily, the walk took only about 45 minutes. The pineapple in my backpack was getting heavy.

The walk heralded the final stretch in the journey from San Cristóbal. Early that morning we had bargained with a taxi driver for the four-hour drive to Yajalón. Our departure was delayed because the driver, Pedro, first stopped to buy extra oil and then he drove to his house to let his wife know that he would be gone all day. En route, not more than 20 minutes later, he pulled off the highway onto a dirt road. When asked why the detour, he matter-of-factly replied that his was a "pirate taxi" and he was avoiding the checkpoint that could require him to stop and produce papers. The detour wasn't long and soon we were back on the highway. While Pedro maneuvered the constant curves and "topes" (speed bumps), I alternatively ate crystallized ginger to quell the nausea and pleaded with him to slow down. I am never comfortable with passing on curves in the mountains, but it seems that taxi drivers thrive on it. As we descended in elevation, the air blowing on us became warmer and more humid.

Linda and I felt it important to visit as many of the member communities of the women's cooperative as we could, and we hadn't yet been to the one in the mountains overlooking Yajalón. Our husbands had accompanied us on this end-of-the-year trip and had somewhat enthusiastically joined us for this excursion. Yajalón is completely off the tourism radar and as we entered the city of about 25,000, I was pleasantly surprised by the clean, attractive buildings. We were met in the city by Fernanda, who would lead us up the mountain to the remote community. We said our good-byes to Pedro and followed Fernanda to the pickup truck that would carry us up the mountain.

We were the only passengers. Sitting on a plank seat in the covered bed of the vehicle, our only view was to the rear. The road was very dusty and the dust flew in every crack and crevice, drying out our eyes and mouths. We held on to anything we could reach as the truck seemingly flew around the curves of the road. When we could no longer proceed due to road construction, there was no alternative except to walk the remaining mile or so. After promising to pick us up at 5 p.m., the young driver turned his truck around and disappeared in a cloud of dust.

The community we were visiting consists of several families. We saw a small primary school and a small store that was teeming with pasta, rice, beans and hair gel. When we arrived, we were greeted by several women who were not just waiting for us but also cooking our lunch. Ducks, turkeys, chickens and children were running around as we ate the welcome meal of pineapple and rice with squash, beans and corn tortillas.

Only one of our scholarship girls hailed from this community but she was in Yajalón where the secondary school was located. We were donating a solar light to the community because electricity is not dependable and most buildings have one light bulb at most. I had hoped to at least look presentable for the presentation. Instead I was sweaty, sticky and caked with the dust from the truck. No sooner had we eaten than we realized that there was an issue that needed resolving. Anita, our scholarship girl, had not been complying with the community service part of her scholarship. Her mother, Evangelina, insisted that they knew nothing of the 100 hours of community service per year that scholarship recipients agree to donate to the cooperative. This was now the middle of year two, and Anita had logged in only four hours of service. Anita was lodging with a "patrona" who received a stipend to house her in Yajalón close to the school. In addition to the controversy around the service hours, mother Evangelina requested more money for school supplies.

My function at this point was to make sure I had enough details to take back to our coordinator in San Cristóbal so an informed decision could be made. I indicated that I would like to speak to Anita when we went back down the mountain into Yajalón. Evangelina decided to accompany us so she could advocate for her daughter. The walk back to the site of the road construction was much more pleasant ... cooler and downhill. The boy with the pickup arrived only a few minutes late, and the views from the cab of the truck were stunning.

The situation became more charged when Anita showed up at Fernanda's house. Fernanda was adamant that a contract had been made in order for Anita to be granted the scholarship and that it was not being fulfilled. Overcome at first by shyness,

Anita did not want to talk, but soon we had an idea that living with the "patrona" was causing a number of issues. First, Anita seemed enamored of western dress and had shed her huipil for a tee shirt. Second, the "patrona" was taking advantage of having the young girl stay with her and was requiring babysitting and other household chores. She had initially refused Anita permission to see us today. I explained to the 14-year-old that I was only a messenger, that any conflict would be resolved by the cooperative and that I had faith in the fairness of its members. At last Anita said she wanted to continue her education and would begin her community service the next Saturday. We parted on good terms.

It was late in the day when we returned to our hotel. One sign that Yajalón was not on the gringo circuit was the interest that Linda and I and our two, tall, bearded husbands generated on the street. One man who could not take his eyes off us narrowly missed walking into a lamppost. After dinner, we all went gratefully to bed. It had been a day filled with driving, walking, visiting, and the rather tense situation of Anita and her mother. My stamina, or rather the lack thereof, kept reminding me of my age. Traveling at 60 requires a few modifications.

Linda and I had a lot of time to talk on the way home. From Yajalón to Ocosingo, we used public combis. Alongside the highway that bypasses Ocosingo, we grabbed breakfast in one of the basic restaurants that attract hungry travelers. We then walked up the road to where the vans leave for San Cristóbal. The van filled quickly but, surprisingly, didn't leave. Our driver was engrossed in conversation with several other men. Patience is a Mexican virtue: waiting engenders no complaints, no whining.

"Well," the driver explained when finally he poked his head in the side door, "this trip is going to cost 70 pesos instead of 30.

We have to take the long way around to San Cristóbal, probably at least an hour more, because a community between Ocosingo and San Cristóbal has blocked the road and vehicles are being held hostage." He further clarified that such blockages are a way to make money and can be profitable at least until the Federales arrive. All but one passenger agreed to the higher fare ($6 instead of $2.50.) An elderly señor descended slowly from the van, clutching his hat, saying that his trip could be postponed a day, thus saving him the extra fare.

After yesterday's pirate taxi, and the combi this morning jammed with 18 passengers, Linda's husband, Tim, commented that it seemed we were embarking on the most efficient ride of them all. The van was big, not overcrowded, and although it was the hottest part of the day, the air from the open windows kept us comfortable.

But Tim had spoken too soon. It wasn't long before the driver stopped to put air in the tires. Then he stopped again for gas. Just after we passed the Maya ruins of Toniná, we were flagged to the side of the road by a policeman and the driver jumped out and walked around to the back of the van. Among the four of us speculation ran rampant. Did the driver not have correct papers? Was there an issue with the van itself? Was it another drug or arms check? Bob, keeping his eye on the rearview mirror, saw money changing hands, and the driver, now a bit poorer, nodded at the policeman and walked a bit dejectedly back to the van.

After an hour or more we turned onto a dirt road and we bumped and jiggled along through the beautiful mountainous scenery. Another half an hour passed and we emerged onto a newly constructed, not yet open road, and on we went, finally coming into the town of Chanal where the road at long last joined the highway to San Cristóbal. Between the wrist pressure bands and the ginger candies, my stomach had behaved. "All in all," I silently congratulated myself, "a good trip."

Postscript: Several months later we learned that Anita's scholarship had been rescinded. She had not shown up for community service and seemed less interested in school. Because she didn't fulfill the obligations of the scholarship, she lost it. This is the only time that has happened and her community leader and the cooperative coordinator made the decision. Although we lost Anita, I was pleased that the cooperative leaders could make tough decisions and that there were consequences for breaking a contract. Anita and her mother had been advised of the terms, and then Anita still had had a chance to make good on her promise. When she didn't do it, trust was broken.

Snapshot number 2:

About an hour and a half south of San Cristóbal lies the city of Comitán. Twenty years ago it was called the City of the Plastic Shoes because along the highway mounds of plastic shoes of all colors were piled high waiting to be sold. In this climate, at quite a bit lower elevation and thus warmer than San Cristóbal, I couldn't imagine wearing such shoes over bare feet, as the indigenous women do.

Comitán, the last major city as you head south to the Guatemala border, has come a long way. The grass-covered median along the highway that runs through the city has huge, impressive sculptures representing the states of Mexico. Comitán is the gateway to Los Lagos de Montebello, la Cascada de Chiflón and other tourist attractions.

A few days after our two-day journey to Yajalón, Linda and I, sans husbands, travelled to visit another group of women who are members of the cooperative. This group is a bit different. They speak a less common Maya language. They don't live in the mountains and they don't wear traditional dress. Because of the warmer climate, the wool cortes (wrap-around skirts) and the heavy woven shawls are not needed. Moreover, this flat land between the highlands and the Guatemala border was home to many fincas — large ranches owned by upper-class landowners — where the indigenous people lived and worked in a system that combined the "company store" concept used by mining communities in the United States and the slavery system in the South. Indigenous people provided the labor force and children were put to work at very early ages. The women under this indentured servitude system did not weave, and traditional clothing did not survive.

The women live in the town of Las Margaritas. The combi ride from Comitán took only about 15 minutes and dropped us off in a pleasant square with a freshly painted church. A walk of another 10 minutes, with a quick stop to pick up fruit and chiles, brought us to the door of the building used by the women. This group differs in another significant way. They are the only group whose members neither weave nor sew. Instead, they have a grinder and grind corn.

Our main objectives were to pay a courtesy visit, to have the chance to chat with the women, and to become better acquainted with Concepción, one of our scholarship recipients who had just completed her second year with us. Her father, a mariachi, very friendly and supportive of his daughter's education, accompanied her. Many of the girls on scholarship don't have fathers, so it was delightful to talk with him. This particular group had put a lot of effort into workshops and into dealing with human rights issues. They had coordinated with the priest of the Catholic Church so as to be able to reach larger audiences. Human rights in particular sparked the attention of 16-year-old Concepción and her goal was to become a human-rights attorney. She worked hard in school and had the advantage of a specific goal to motivate her.

Over a lunch of chicken in mole and rice, the group spoke of a series of workshops they wanted to present especially to outlying communities that have few opportunities for workshop participation. They promised to send us a proposal, and we promised to take it under consideration.

Rosa also addressed us. She was raised in the finca system and thus had no schooling at all. She had been hoping for a long time to take an evening course so she could complete her primary education, something we knew we could support. Linda remarked on how well the women worked together and supported each other and it was not the first time that we were similarly impressed. Solidarity is strong here.

Postscript 1

- *Concepción finished preparatory school and in the fall of 2011 entered university to study law. She became ill during the second semester with typhoid and missed too many classes to continue. She plans to continue studying, but has decided not to pursue her law degree at this time.*
- *With our support, Rosa completed the adult equivalent course of primary school education and she is now working on her secondary certificate.*
- *We approved the series of seven workshops proposed by the women of Las Margaritas. People were recruited from outlying communities to attend and then carry the information back to their villages. Workshops lasted two days, had professional presenters, and covered topics such as domestic violence, gender equity, human rights, justice in Mexico and self-esteem. In July, 2009, Linda and I returned to Las Margaritas to attend the "gender equity" workshop. Twenty-five people were in atten-*

dance. Eva, the head of the women's group, did a great job of facilitating the workshop and of making it comfortable and safe for participation. She talked of "planting seeds for the future," because gender equity doesn't happen overnight. Women related problems due to the "macho" culture and the constant struggle for their voices to be heard. The fact that four men attended and regularly shared their own views lent hope to the process and gave encouragement to the women attending. As educators ourselves, we found the workshop dynamic, thoughtful and well-organized, high praise indeed. The materials for all seven workshops were compiled into packets so that they would serve as guidelines for those who would repeat the workshops in other venues. Once the women have some resources, the stage is set for transformation.

Postscript 2

After Linda and I were so impressed with Eva's skill at workshop facilitation and her organizational prowess, we were bowled over to find out that she was illiterate. She subsequently requested funding from us so she could complete her primary school certificate in night school. We were more than pleased to help, and she completed the course.

In 2011, the abovementioned Eva, always outspoken and forthright, especially when compared with the traditionally shy, less assertive, cooperative members, sported a tee shirt that surprised me. It read: "SEX when I desire it … PREGNANCY when I decide."

SCHOLARSHIP GIRLS

The Maya culture is rich in so many ways. Preserving this culture, along with the many languages, is extremely important. The difficulty exists in the precarious balance between keeping the culture and at the same time utilizing and/or taking advantage of some of modernity's contributions. The Otavalans in Ecuador are an example of an indigenous people who have struck such a balance. Their success lies in how much they value and preserve their traditions and at the same time operate shrewdly in the current economic market.

Teenage girls in any culture encompass a range of maturity levels, vary in their ability to set long-term goals and can be affected positively or negatively by their peers. The girls we support are the same, giggling in the corner, shyly meeting our eyes or giving us hugs that have increased in duration and meaning as they know us over the years. And yet, this generation of girls is more aware of that fine line between the honoring and the keeping of tradition, and the desire to break away from it.

Is there any such thing as a "normal" teenager? Indigenous girls in Chiapas create new fashion designs and colors within the parameters of their native dress. They are interested in the latest gossip, and there are some who sport cell phones. It is still not unusual to be married by 14 with babies rapidly on the way. It is also not unusual to think that their lives will be much like their mother's and grandmother's: tending the house, making the tortillas, carrying water, and weaving. But faster communication and more exposure to the world outside of small communities is having its effect, for better or for worse.

Mujeres de Maiz OF has no agenda except to provide the resources for women, girls and children to continue their education. What we have seen is that girls and women take what they learn and invest it back into their communities. Josefa in Zinacantán is teaching computer skills to the children, giving back what she has learned and thus serving as a role model to the younger set. Children are not accustomed to seeing girls and women from their own communities in positions of authority. Given the opportunity to attend computer classes or our Saturday Program, boys and girls gain respect for their teachers and begin to see them as individuals with skills and talents. Women don't have to be servants in their own houses under a man's thumb. Girls begin to have dreams: "I can be a teacher," "I'm interested in nursing," or realize that they can be community leaders once they are literate. And boys learn that one day a wife can be a more equal partner.

Felisa applied for a scholarship and began preparatory school, which is the equivalent of our 10th grade. With her winning smile and willingness to take on a quarter share of responsibility for the Saturday Children's Program in her community, we were more than happy to have her aboard. In her second year she met a boy. She was just turning 17. She was Catholic, and the boy was Protestant. This is serious business in the communities as the religions mix at their peril. About a month before the school year ended, Felisa ran off with the boy and went to live with his family. Her family essentially disowned her and she dropped out of school. She also withdrew from the cooperative. Within a few months she was safely married to her young man but still estranged from her family.

I was apprised of this turn of events by Ramona, the coordinator of the cooperative and our liaison in Chiapas. We were sorry to lose Felisa and sorrier to hear of the familial rift. At the next bi-monthly workshop, her sister Patricia approached me and related the story again. I was pleased that she told me herself and then I realized why. With hesitating words she asked, "So now that Felisa no longer attends classes, do we need to pay you back for all her expenses so far?" Knowing that their mother is a poor widow with six children, I could just imagine their discussing this and worrying that somehow a non-completion of a school year would incur penalties. "Of course not," I reassured her. "We are sorry that Felisa didn't finish her second year on scholarship, but we look at it this way. She has essentially two more years of education than she would have without the scholarship. We feel that that in itself is valuable." Patricia's relief was palpable.

The following year, Patricia herself was in the "problem spotlight." It seems that when she was a baby she had been dropped on her head and had suffered headaches ever since. They seemed to be worse when she was in school, and this fact was communicated to Ramona, who wrote to me right away. After a quick consultation with the board, I responded that we'd pay for her medical bills if she'd consent to see a doctor. We also brainstormed possible reasons why the headaches were particularly bad in school: Perhaps the lighting was bad, perhaps there were allergens in the walls, perhaps it was the stress, or perhaps she wanted to stop going to school and this would provide the rationale.

Ramona took her to the doctor and vitamins were prescribed and some tests were run and her headaches lessened in severity. Within a few months, however, Patricia decided not to continue her scholarship the following year. And that was her decision. Our role is to respect individuals and their decisions, and again, Patricia had two more years of education than she would have received otherwise. On a personal level, I was sorry to lose both sisters. They were personable and bright.

Patricia and Felisa were not the only girls we "lost." I previously mentioned Anita, the young girl in Yajalón who was perhaps influenced by the ladino culture where she was boarding, or perhaps was a bit immature and could not as yet recognize the value of education. And then there was Carmela, who just after being awarded the scholarship had to forego it to take care of her older sister who was ill and bedridden. Another girl dropped her scholarship after having a baby. And another stopped after she completed secondary school. These things happen. Some education is better than none. There is no argument about that.

Most of the scholarship recipients have continued their studies. Since we as an organization are only in our seventh year, we'll see how this goes. But results are certainly encouraging as we see the same girls back again, year after year, showing more self-confidence, more inclination to share their opinions and knowing that they are capable.

THE ZINACANTÁN SATURDAY CHILDREN´S PROGRAM

Toward the end of 2009, the four scholarship recipients from the community of Zinacantán had an idea. Josefa, majoring in computer science at the university level, had been given a job teaching computer skills to the Zinacanteco children. Her eyes lit up when she talked about it. She and her sister and two other girls on scholarship with us got together and hammered out a proposal. They wanted to help the primary school children who were struggling in school, were getting left behind, and were ultimately dropping out. They approached the primary school teachers for recommendations of students and started their program with about 30 participants from ages 4 to 10.

The proposal submitted to us consisted of a full-year plan. Topics would include strengthening academic skills such as reading, math and writing; developing creativity; reading and writing in Tsotsil, their Maya language; environmental stewardship; and workshops emphasizing gender equity, self-esteem, children's rights, and the like. The "class" would meet every Saturday for three hours and a meal would be provided. Materials needed and the expense of certified instructors for certain workshops were included in the cost proposal. An outline for each Saturday was mapped out. To measure progress, an assessment of each topic was included.

The board and I were knocked out by the proposal. Not only would this satisfy the requirements for community service on the part of the four scholarship girls who had conceived of the program and would run it, but it would supplement education to primary school children at risk for leaving school early. We funded it at the 90 percent level. As a small organization, we have to be careful that the women in the cooperative don't think that we are made of money. The money we have is all fundraised. And we knew that the program would be a "go" at that level of funding.

The Saturday classes started immediately. Ramona made sure to visit regularly and check in. I visited the program twice in the first year and this is what I saw:

- A group of very engaged, participating children
- A puppet show featuring handmade stick puppets talking about values in community life such as friendship, loyalty, etc.
- Hand-written, original stories in Spanish (their second language) that the children themselves read aloud to us
- Younger children working on drawing shapes in preparation to writing
- Older children playing bingo using their multiplication skills
- An exercise that taught writing in Tsotsil
- The individual creation of Spanish-Tsotsil dictionaries
- A hot meal at the end of the morning
- A notebook put together at the end of the workshop that dealt with children's rights. The children had thought about what they had learned, wrote down the rights that were important to them, and then drew a corresponding picture.

Excerpts: (my translation):

a. "The right to education. I like to go to school because I want to read so that I understand a lot."

b. "The right to play."

c. "The right to have a family."

d. "The right to education. I like to read, write and draw."

e. "The right to play sports because I like to play basketball with my friends." (written by a girl)

f. "The right to education. I like to go to school because I like to do multiplication but sometimes I don't like school because my teacher hits me."

g. "The right to study, to play at recess, to write, draw and paint."

h. "The right to education when my teacher doesn't pull my ear."

You get the idea.

The program is now in its third year (as of February 2012) and is flourishing. Some children have moved on and others have joined. Parents have commented that they are hearing fewer complaints from the primary school teachers and that their children are having more success in the classroom. This is an amazing program and we are proud to fund it.

THE CRUCERO SATURDAY CHILDREN'S PROGRAM: DECEMBER, 2010

December in San Cristóbal is really quite pleasant, especially if you have arrived there from the Pacific Northwest. Most days the sky is an intense blue and only occasionally are there clouds or light rain. But as Ramona and I climbed in elevation to the community of Crucero, the fog came in and with it a chilly drizzle in the misty air.

When I visited Crucero in the summer of 2009, I was amazed at the changes from two years previous. At that time we walked on a dirt track to the community, which lies about a 40-minute trek from the highway. But since then a road has been built and humble houses have been constructed alongside. The feel was different, more accessible yet less removed and peaceful. Progress, I have learned, is usually a mix of positive and negative. Two steps forward, one step back, perhaps.

Inside the small building that normally serves as the common sewing room for the women in the community who belong to Mujeres de Maíz en Resistencia, were 13 children and their two teachers. Frida and Manuela, both 16, were in their fourth year of our scholarship program. After the Saturday Children´s

Program began a year ago in Zinacantán, these two girls decided to emulate it as part of their community service requirement.

Ramona and I entered the one-room building and 13 faces turned toward us, smiling at Ramona and looking a bit more inquisitively at me. The girls and boys were from the second to the fourth grades, although ages don't always correspond to level. They were in the middle of a lesson on math, taught mainly by Frida. Manuela was walking around the small tables, putting check marks on correct answers.

"Usually there are up to 22 students," Frida informed us, "but today the rain has kept them home." All the students were bundled up in layers of clothing. I noticed that the corrugated tin roof had broken over the far wall and a fair amount of water was coming in, soaking the handicraft stuffed animals on a shelf.

After introductions all around, Frida continued the lesson. The children willingly worked on the addition, subtraction, multiplication and division problems that she doled out. I couldn't help but marvel that this was *Saturday* and these children came to this three-hour class voluntarily.

After a few minutes I started to help Manuela monitor the answers and help the students who were having difficulties. But my ability to help was limited as I found out that while numbers are in Spanish, procedural explanations were in Tsotsil. At this age level, the children are not yet bi-lingual. The class continued as Frida challenged the children with some problems done on the white board. If the children struggled, she talked them through it. Every child had to go the board.

When I met Frida and Manuela for the first time in 2007, they were painfully shy. When they answered a question, their voices were barely audible. And now, here they were, running this class, not intimidated at all by my gringa presence. When

I had the chance to talk to them a bit, I found that Frida most enjoyed her classes of science and reading while Manuela preferred science and history.

We are delighted with the Saturday programs. The scholarship girls, who organize and teach many of the lessons, are becoming role models to the younger children, who rarely see young women in leadership roles. If the lessons are beyond their level of expertise, credentialed teachers are brought in to present topics. The proposal, modeled after the Zinacantán program, included all themes for the year-long program including evaluation techniques. The children receive a meal before they go home. Every child has a plastic bag with his/her own materials: a pencil, a small notebook. We fund it all, including the white boards, markers and the child-size tables and chairs.

The school room was cold and damp. Hmmm, I thought, perhaps we should invest in a heater for the children. I mentioned the idea to Ramona, and she immediately dismissed the idea. The kids shouldn't get warm and then have to leave and go out in the cold and return to a cold house. The changes in temperature are not good for their health, she informed me. I was so glad I hadn't arbitrarily bought and presented them with a heater. They would have thanked me politely and the heater would have been pushed in a corner, unused and a waste of money.

Mujeres de Maiz Opportunity Foundation is proud that the women assess their own needs. Our assumptions, derived from another culture, practically another century, would be not only presumptuous, but in many cases, totally off base.

THE CRUCERO SATURDAY CHILDREN'S PROGRAM: PART TWO, AUGUST, 2011

In August, 2011, Linda and I were invited to Crucero on a Saturday. The Children's Program was finishing its first year and we had been invited, along with the parents of the children who attended, to an end-of-year presentation. The 40-minute taxi drive over, we walked the 2 kilometers to where the cooperative meets. It was a warm day, sunny and bright, and the walk was pleasant.

When we arrived, we hardly recognized the place. Not only had a fence been built, but there was a new structure that backed onto the road. It consisted of wooden plank walls, a corrugated plastic roof, a dirt floor and the typical single lightbulb hanging from the ceiling.

After our greetings with the women in the community, I asked about the new building. "Go inside," we were urged. It was a bit dark until our eyes adapted to the dim light. Along two walls sat 20 children, ranging in age from 5 to 12, all holding notebooks in their laps. Each notebook contained an original story that the child had written. All sat patiently, expectantly. The tables we had funded were piled to one side to make room for chairs for guests. Linda and I looked at each other. This building had sprung up since my last visit seven months earlier. The community had worked together to build it, to provide a space for the Saturday Children's Program. It was an amazing moment for us.

After a few minutes and the arrival of more parents, the program started. As each name was called, the child would stand and read his/her story. The teachers, Frida, Manuela and Andrea, a new scholarship recipient, followed along on their own copies in case prompting was necessary. Today, the boys seemed more timid than the girls. One needed to be coaxed; another shifted his weight from side to side while he read. One girl kept her folder covering her face the entire time she read, and my photo shows a pink folder with legs in blue pants. The older children wrote in both Spanish and their native Tsotsil. Literacy in Tsotsil, not taught in primary schools, is part of the Saturday curriculum. The younger ones who hadn't yet learned to write in Tsotsil, wrote just in Spanish, and the tiny ones had drawn pictures that they would explain. Each child received applause, and Linda and I were free with compliments and praise.

Immediately afterward we were invited to stay for a meal. All would be fed. As two women carried in a giant cauldron of soup filled with vegetables, Linda took pictures of the children and their families. These would later be sent to Ramona who would print and distribute them. The soup was dished out and served. It was a joyous occasion for all concerned.

Before we left, one of the children's mothers approached us. We know her well. She is a mover and shaker in the cooperative. We have grown to respect her zeal and her organizational skills.

"How long will you be able to fund this program?" she asks. A very good question, right to the point. A dedicated space for the program had been constructed. The parents are happy with it, as are the children.

I'd like nothing better than to make guarantees ... "as long as you want the program," "years," "forever." But we can't. Our word is our bond here and we have vowed to be honest and forthright at all times. "The program is funded for the next year," I reply. "And after that, it depends on the success of our fundraising. We will do our best."

She nods. We take our leave, humbled by the experience and at the same time delighted and uplifted. How lucky we are.

A CHALLENGE FROM THE INSIDE: ALCOHOLISM AND DOMESTIC VIOLENCE

Anyone who has visited the indigenous communities around San Cristobal has seen the men passed out on the church steps, or in the square or at the side of the road. It's a risky proposition, given the propensity to alcoholism on the part of indigenous people, to then imbue their spiritual rituals with the potent, fermented sugarcane juice called posh. Shamans use posh (from the Tsotsil "*pox-il*" which means "healing") in ceremonies to cure illnesses. Imbibing the strong liquor creates the trance state necessary to bridge the gap between this world and the spiritual realm in which the shaman can better ascertain how to deal with the illness or emotional distress that he has been called on to cure.

Addiction is easy, and countless men die young due to alcoholism. Several of the girls on scholarship have witnessed the early deaths of their fathers. The widows of these men many times choose not to remarry. Carrying on alone is difficult but more advisable than putting oneself back under the thumb of another alcoholic. The women themselves rarely drink.

I brought this topic up with Ramona and she told me that the women had participated in a workshop about alcoholism.

I wondered aloud if they were familiar with Al-Anon and she didn't think so. After a bit of research on the web, I proposed to Ramona that Al-Anon present a workshop. Women might know what alcoholism was but learning how to live with it and not be enablers is quite different. I was surprised to learn that there are a number of Al-Anon meetings in San Cristóbal. (I had noticed on my forays around town many venues for AA, and several for "Neurotics Anonymous.") Ramona arranged for two women to give a workshop at one of the bi-monthly reunions of the cooperative. I was fortunate to be there at the time.

The speakers, Adela and Marta, were not indigenous. They began by telling their own stories, how they had tried to manage a home with an alcoholic husband and how they tried to protect their children. They explained how they had been embarrassed to talk about their situation. And then they described the help afforded to them by Al-Anon, and the dramatic improvement in their lives. The women listened attentively but only one or two volunteered to share experiences. The trust level wasn't there yet. I thought that what the presenters shared was powerful. Before they left, they gave addresses and times of local Al-Anon meetings.

What happened after they left I attribute to Ramona's skill at debriefing and extending the discussion. She re-capped and began to draw the women out. Soledad admitted that not only was her husband an alcoholic, but several of her sons were also addicted to the bottle. Rigoberta confessed that before her husband died he used to hit her. Another shared that as soon as she received her monthly government stipend of approximately $20, her husband took it from her to buy alcohol. Several more copied down the information about the meetings.

I suggested to Ramona that a follow-up meeting with the same women might prove valuable. She agreed. In a macho society it's doubly hard for the women to rebel against their husbands. The consequences can be physical injury or worse. And there is essentially no legal recourse. The members of the cooperative know they are not alone. Belonging in itself lends them strength and provides them with support.

CHALLENGES FROM THE OUTSIDE

The women of the cooperative are amazing: hard-working, resilient, wise, and curious. Over the years as trust has grown, their eyes now meet ours, they ask direct questions, and hugs are longer and stronger. One of the things I most admire about the women is that they embody regional diversity. Some are traditional Catholics, some are Maya-Catholics, some are Protestants. Three Maya languages are represented. While most of their communities are located in the mountains, a few lie in the sub-tropics. Some are Zapatista leaning, others are not. And yet they work and laugh together, putting aside their differences so they can learn and problem-solve and find strength in common struggles.

In August, 2011, Linda and I filmed testimonials from seven of our scholarship girls. All those interviewed had been with us at least two years and of course we filmed Iliana, our first scholarship recipient, now in her sixth year and closing in on her graduation from university.

We formulated about 20 questions and sent them to Ramona ahead of our trip so she could distribute them to the girls. This would give them time to think about their answers. We were hoping for elaboration in their responses, and that's what we got. Despite being a bit shy with the camcorder running, the responses were lengthy and complete. Tears came to Josefa's eyes as she expressed gratitude at the end of her interview. It was an emotional moment and I teared up as well, so proud of her efforts and persistence.

Iliana is an English major and yet, over the years, she remained shy about speaking to us. Linda would attempt to draw out a response in English and Iliana would give very short or one-word answers, intimidated about speaking in front of native speakers. I approached her just before we taped her and asked her if she'd be interested in doing the interview in English. I almost fell over when she replied in the affirmative. As she answered our questions in English, my heart swelled. What a privilege to be part of the "leg up" in the education of these young women! How fortunate I am to lead this organization! The compassion and strength that I see in the Virgin of Guadalupe's face came to mind, and I realize that my gratitude is directed, almost unconsciously, to her.

Every time I visit the cooperative, I learn more about the obstacles facing the women. There are the large, rather nebulous challenges of racism, sexism and poverty. These clouds are always present. But the more specific obstacles may be even more insidious and difficult to counter. A list of these obstacles, by no means complete, follows:

- The pressure is on by producers of genetically modified seed to sell the seed. The women are aware that it doesn't re-seed and needs to be purchased annually. There have been issues of such seed blowing into adjacent corn fields and contaminating the existing seed.
- Multi-national corporations are buying up mineral rights. Many times the minerals are next to or under an existing community. "Rural cities" are being built and indigenous people are being forced and / or bribed into leaving their

land and moving into the government-sponsored villages. This has already happened in at least two places that I know of. The promises made by the government are already not being fulfilled. In one of the rural cities, the government sponsored chili cultivation. The growers wanted to take the chilis to market but were told that a company in Canada would pay triple the price and were urged to wait for that deal. The sale didn't go through, the chilis rotted, and all revenue was lost.

- Mines for copper or other minerals poison the local water. Rights Action, a non-profit group based in Toronto, follows the horrifying accounts of mines established principally in Latin American countries. The corporations, with impunity, visit all kinds of crimes (including murder and rape) and deceit upon the local populace.

- The government sponsors certain crops, many not native to the region. An example is the Palma Africana, grown for combustible fuels. The people who agree to grow it receive a certain amount of money monthly but once Palma Africana is grown, nothing else will thrive in that soil.

- Infrastructure is being expanded throughout Chiapas. It is not being built for the convenience of anything except the large corporations that need reliable roads. One of the women in the cooperative complained that a road was built right through her community and some people lost their houses. There had been no notice of this and there was no recourse.

- Hydroelectric dams are proposed on major rivers, including the Usumacinta, which is the longest river in Central America. Piedras Negras, an archeological site founded in 300 BC, as well as 18 other sites, are threatened by one such dam and could end up lost forever underwater. Moreover, indigenous communities are displaced by dams.

- Water rights are being bought up. This has been going on for years. Coca-Cola is one of the largest offenders. Indigenous peoples have had free water for centuries and now have to contend with large faceless corporations charging them for water use.

- Military bases, presumably to protect the Guatemala border and to contend with drug trafficking, are positioned around villages, particularly those that declare themselves autonomous. The soldiers are guilty of harassment and low-intensity warfare tactics to intimidate the indigenous. As of this writing, there are 60 military bases in Chiapas.

- Corruption is rife. Judges are in the politician's pockets. According to Frayba (Fray Bartolomé de las Casas Center for Human Rights) there were as many as 15 to 20 cases of torture in 2011.

- The North American Free Trade Agreement (NAFTA) has caused problems for the indigenous and working class. The cheap corn crossing from the U.S. has undersold the corn raised on the tiny milpas in the indigenous villages. Malnutrition has gone up significantly in recent years as people cannot compete with the cheap corn flooding the markets.

How can indigenous women, who are powerless in society, de-humanized and marginalized, address such huge issues that have potentially devastating impacts? How can they make themselves heard?

The women with whom we partner are learning they have worth. They have voices. They have opinions that need to be heard. Education is but one piece of the puzzle, but it's an essential one. Through workshops and school programs and participation the women are finding their voices. They are learning that in a global society, they have a place that merits respect. Their dedication to organic farming, their interest in projects that help the environment, their participation in campaigns to end domestic violence, their amazing creativity and their dreams for their children, will eventually earn them that respect. But it's a long, hard road.[9]

---

[9] See appendix "Chiapas in 2011 ...." by Miguel Picard

FUNDRAISING

If anyone had told me that I'd be fundraising as an adjunct to running a non-profit organization, I would have stated in no uncertain terms that fundraising was not for me. I was wrong. I have found fundraising to take many forms that are challenging, satisfying and completely surprising. *Mujeres* has a great board. The eight (our board grew by two members as of June, 2012) of us have different strengths and of course different life paths, so we have different constraints and priorities on our time.

As Board Chair and pretty much the impetus behind *Mujeres*, I had to embrace fundraising. From grant writing, to contacting people in person, to writing our annual solicitation letter, to public speaking ... I learned by doing.

In theory, it's uncomfortable to ask for money. But the discomfort factor vanishes for me when the request is in aid of work that I am passionate about. Asking for donations affords people the opportunity to give of themselves and thus makes them feel good about their gift. You have to truly believe in what you are doing and you have to know, beyond any doubt, that people like themselves better when they give to others.

So here's how the fundraising goes. I'm going to talk about what we do, and what I do, in the following list.

1. Annual event
2. Funds solicitation letter
3. Local organizations
4. Church support
5. Garage sale
6. Grants
7. Local fundraisers
8. Daily activities and the fastest donation ever

Annual event: We have established an annual event to rec-ognize El Día de los Muertos, (Day of the Dead), celebrated on November 1 and 2 in Latin America. We put on a dinner and silent/live auction. We rent the local Grange Hall on the Saturday nearest the above dates. One of our board members, Molly, is a great cook and has lots of experience cooking for crowds. She is invaluable in this respect and is in charge of the dinner in all its aspects. Here is where I literally (well, almost) stay out of the kitchen. A vegetarian Mexican dinner is prepared and we normally feed about 110 people. Some of the food is donated to us from a local organic farm. The 110 diners pay a suggested donation of $20. We make it clear that we don't turn anyone away due to lack of funds. We provide a bit of music during dinner. Sometimes I talk about Día de los Muertos and the significance it has in Latin American culture. Martha, our board member who is an art teacher and artist herself, brings in an altar that we decorate. Last year we dedicated the altar to the memory of two of our supporters who had passed away. I always talk about what *Mujeres* has done in the previous year and show a Power Point or a short video. We have an extraor-dinary selection of handicrafts, clothing, jewelry and weavings from Chiapas for our silent auction, as well as donations from local artists and supporters. A live auction of a few selected very special items follows the dinner.

Living in a small community is helpful, I think, and now, after six of these events we have a loyal, solid group of attendees. Newspaper and radio coverage bring in some new folks. It requires a down and dirty, full-out blast of energy to put this on. The hall isn't available until the morning of the event. The day is spent in food preparation, decorating and setting up and laying out the auction items. The event starts at 5:30 and is over by 8. The hall is cleaned and packed up by 10:30 at night. Leftover food goes to local centers for the homeless. I return to the hall at 9 the following morning with all their kitchen towels washed. Then most of us go into full zombie-mode for the next two days.

Annual solicitation letter: Once a year we send out a fund-raiser letter. I try to think of a distinct approach each year. I talk about where the money will go. We send out a return envelope, unstamped. Our mailing list is about 300 people. I would say we usually get about a 20-percent response. I read somewhere that the big charities consider a 10-percent response to be good.

Local organizations: Local organizations are terrific. Just check what your local Soroptimist and Rotary clubs do. It's amazing and impressive. They have a lot of demands on their time and on their resources. They also need a speaker at almost every meeting. So I have called just about every club in the area and volunteered a 20-minute talk. At the beginning I just presented *Mujeres* and told what we did. Now I always make a point to ask for their help. After I have spoken, I send them proposals, ideas and ways in which they could help us. You don't get what you don't ask for. This I have learned. Soroptimist International of Sequim adopted our cause when we were 4 months old and hadn't as yet been notified by the IRS of our legal status. Because we are dealing with girls and women and education, we were a great fit for their international cause. They have supported us ever since. *Mujeres* shows up monthly in their newsletter, thanks to a great contact within their club. And in December, 2011, we finally had a Soroptimist representative come to Chiapas to see our work firsthand. That representative then graciously accepted our proposal to join our board as treasurer. We now have an official link between our organizations. Yes!

The local Sunrise Rotary has been extremely supportive. I've talked to them several times. We just received our first check from a Kiwanis group. Beta Nu, PEO and AAUW have invited me to speak and have given us contributions. Follow-up is important and here is one area where our secretary is so important. Thank-you notes need to be personal and timely. In addition I write progress letters and will e-mail extra thank-yous.

I feel it is very important to keep *Mujeres'* name in front of people's noses so they know that we are always working and we are not forgotten or overlooked. Recently we have become part of a small group of NGO's meeting in Seattle. We share the same principles. Talking to other non-profits generates lots of ideas.

Churches: One of the first questions people ask when they hear about us is if we are missionaries. The answer, I've found, depends on the definition of the word itself. Many religious organizations do a tremendous amount of good. But I prefer that "doing good" stand on its own and not be related with proselytizing. I've read accounts where handouts and help were nothing more than bribery schemes for conversion. Cortez and his henchman Francisco de Alvarado killed indigenous people by the thousands, saving tortured souls for His Most Catholic Majesties and for Spain, and opening the floodgates to missionaries all over Latin America. My Unitarian upbringing suggested that there are many paths to the same goal, and I am convinced of that. Respect and tolerance, that's the ticket. OK, that's *my* ticket.

The women in the cooperative are largely Catholic. But "Catholic" varies some from community to community depending on which of the Maya traditions and beliefs survived the heavy trampling of Spanish feet. Many beliefs are combined into fascinating eclectic, spiritual weavings that echo the original weavings themselves. Others in the cooperative are Evangélicas, who were weaned away from the Catholic tradition by persuasive Jehovah's Witnesses, Seventh Day Adventists, Mormons, etc. I am digressing, bear with me.

It is important to *Mujeres* to have the support of religious organizations. We have found that those churches concerned primarily with increasing their own ranks usually don't help groups outside their own religious parameters. But many churches are more concerned with service than with winning converts, and we have been fortunate to garner support from them. Unitarian-Universalist congregations have been extremely generous. Local Methodist and Episcopalian churches extended support. We would love to add to that list.

Garage sale: Once a year we have a garage sale. It's a huge amount of work. Days are spent organizing and pricing. Most of the goods are donated by our supporters. We pride ourselves on a "quality" sale and after several years of doing this, we are getting repeat customers who know we have a great selection of items. The day of the sale is the fun part and includes lots of talking and joking with customers. Most of what doesn't sell goes to local thrift shops. The past year, some leftover furniture went to a local consignment shop. A few items may be worth ads in the classifieds. Surplus books go to our local library's monthly sale.

New 2012 "Men with Guitars" concert: Our newest event, thanks to longtime *Mujeres'* supporter and new board member Steve, was a concert of '50s and '60s music performed at a park clubhouse. Steve invited local musicians to play, booked the hall, and bought beer and wine. Newspaper publicity, flyers around town and e-mails to our supporters brought in a sell-out crowd. The only expenses were the liquor license, the drinks and the hall rental. Everyone raved ... both attendees and musicians alike. This may well become an annual event.

Grants: Grants are tough when economic times are good. When the country is in the middle of the worst recession in decades, grant money dries up. I knew nothing about grants. Nothing. But nothing ventured, nothing gained. Grants take tons of time. If the grant isn't prepared exactly as required, it lands in a round file somewhere and is never even acknowledged. If you want to write grants, this is not the place for advice.

I will tell you two grant stories.

1. I had applied to the Kellogg Foundation and received back a letter of interest asking for much more information. That completed, I sent it and received a reply from Kellogg in Mexico City. The woman sent advice on how to tighten up my proposal and counseled a few changes. I followed her advice. Her recommendations continued over a few days, and I admit I was getting excited. I had never had such hands-on contact and an exchange of messages EVER with a foundation. Finally I had the proposal to her satisfaction and submitted it. In less than 48 hours, I received the generic "no thank you." Disappointment does not begin to address how I felt.

2. Alternative Gifts International showed up on my radar one day when I was researching grants. Publishers of

a catalog showcasing over 30 non-profits, AGI works with organizations and churches to sponsor fairs to garner support for a wide range of organizations. Their premise appealed to me because I like the idea of giving where it's really needed. I love getting cards that say a goat was donated in my name somewhere in Africa, or a donation was made so a girl could go to school. I strongly support the idea that money normally spent on unneeded or unwanted gifts is better spent where it will make a serious difference.

I sent in the proposal to AGI and we were accepted. The first year we shared a page of the catalog with two other organizations. The second and third years we had our own page and the fourth year is just starting with another full page. Proposals have to be sent yearly. But here is the interesting thing: *Mujeres* is a tiny, grassroots foundation, no paid staff, just a working, volunteer board. We represented one of the extremes. The Nature Conservancy was at the other end of the spectrum. Worldwide, hugely respected, tons of paid staff ... TNC is also in the AGI catalog. OK, so a little pride comes in here. We were rubbing shoulders with the big guys! And, one result of "rubbing shoulders" was that a worker with The Nature Conservancy near Tuxtla Gutiérrez in Chiapas gave a workshop on climate change to the women in the cooperative! AGI has been a godsend. Enough said.

You must be ready to jump through hoops for grant monies. The percentage of grants received can be infinitismal to the number of grants applied for. But still, they can make a huge difference.

Local fundraisers: An ex-student of mine who majored in Spanish was surprised to find my name on the *Mujeres* website as she surfed the web looking for organizations. We met and, within a few weeks, she took the initiative and arranged a benefit for us at a local bar. She asked for a voluntary cover charge and ran a raffle of various donations she had requested from local businesses. The bar owner said it was the best night of receipts he'd had in a long time, and we got a check for $607.

My brother-in-law gave me a bottle of 1966 port a few years back. I donated it to *Mujeres* and contacted another ex-student of mine, a young woman who owns the local wine shop. She jumped in immediately and we arranged a silent auction for the bottle with a kick-off night at her store. The port turned out to be quite rare and we ended up with $200.

After speaking about *Mujeres* to a local community college Spanish class, a fiber-arts artist in the class offered to run an online raffle for her art. In a month, she presented us with a check for more than $700.

Sequim proudly hosts an annual Lavender Farm Faire. Non-profit groups, if accepted, may set up a booth for the three-day event. Volunteers helped us fill the time slots and in addition to information and the sale of small items from Chiapas or donated by supporters, we designed a free coloring project for children. Well over $800 was raised during this event. These amounts are huge in love and in the generous thoughts behind them.

Daily activities and the fastest donation ever: *Mujeres* is my passion. I carry *Mujeres* business cards that I pass out when-ever the occasion arises (and sometimes when it doesn't.) I just know that a card I pass out one day will pay off. So when I was waiting for some friends to show up at a local coffee shop, another woman sitting alone and I struck up a conversation about the local lavender festival, the weather and her search for perfect orthotics. Of course the lavender festival topic had to include that *Mujeres* was going to have a booth there and WHAM! I'm on the water slide that ejects me into the pool of *Mujeres* information for the NEW PERSON. After my two minute spiel — I do try not to be overly zealous and move into the boring range — the topic shifted. A moment later, the woman jumped up and came over to me and, apologizing for not having her checkbook, she handed me an envelope full of cash. "I want to make a donation right now," she proclaimed. While I was thanking her profusely, I was also astounded. She didn't know me from Adam, didn't know if *Mujeres* was legitimate, nada. So I frantically found my business card and showed her on her IPAD where our website was and promised her a receipt as soon as I got home. Because the friends I expected had found themselves stalled in traffic due to an accident and had to turn around, the woman and I sat and talked another half hour at least. It was when I got to my car that I ventured a look in the envelope. $100! That was the fastest donation ever. I was so grateful for her impulse and her trust. If my friends had arrived, my connection with her wouldn't have happened. Sometimes the universe just works.

One last word on donations. A goodly number of our supporters are retired and live on fixed incomes. Some donations are $10 or $15. As Linda says, "That's money we didn't have before." And those amounts are significant because amounts are relative. The person who takes the time and interest and cares enough to write out a $10 check from her Social Security, needs to know how valued and valuable he/she is. The larger donations should not overshadow the small ones. Our supporters are all in this together.

AFTERWORD

As the Board Chair and a founding member of *Mujeres de Maiz Opportunity Foundation,* I have found myself in a position to make a small difference. The Board members, all volunteer, support our efforts wholeheartedly. We make small steps, admittedly. But change begins with a small step. My teaching career, which I loved, has parlayed into this wonderful, deserving project: my legacy.

Advice? Only one thing. Find a cause. Start younger than I did and find your passion and apply it to a cause you love. It doesn't matter where. What matters is that you feel the call, the pull, the desire. Step up for those who can't. Be a voice for those who have none. I recommend not having a personal agenda. Let the agenda come from the source. The inner strength of that source will amaze you.

IN A NUTSHELL

Mujeres de Maiz Opportunity Foundation was founded in January, 2006, and has 501(c)(3) status. Our mission statement explains our purpose:

We are dedicated to partnering with and empowering indigenous women in Chiapas, Mexico, by providing them with access to education. Our goal is to help break the cycle of poverty, build self-esteem, and create positive role models.

As of July, 2012, there are 19 young women attending school on our scholarships.

We fund community projects that are education based. We have funded a series of workshops in Las Margaritas. We currently fund two full-year continuing Saturday programs for primary school children in Zinacantán and Crucero. We also are currently funding an adult literacy program in Altamirano. Starting in the fall of 2012 a new project is the funding of composting toilets for 28 families. The project includes workshops regarding health and hygiene issues.

Laptop computers have been donated to each of the 12 communities as well as to Ramona, who as coordinator takes care of both the cooperative's and our business. An additional computer is housed at the cooperative center, where it may be checked out by girls on scholarship on a "library" basis.

We fund a number of workshops for the cooperative's bi-monthly meetings each year.

We provide eye exams and glasses to all who request them. This year alone, 23 women and girls received glasses.

The board members are all volunteers. We pay our own expenses when we travel to Chiapas.

Mujeres De Maiz Opportunity Foundation

www.MujeresDeMaizOF.org

mujeres@olypen.com

Donations are gratefully accepted through our website or may be mailed to P.O. Box 1954, Sequim, WA 98382. Thank you.

After printing expenses, proceeds from this book will be donated to Mujeres de Maiz Opportunity Foundation.

APPENDIX

Letters from Scholarship Recipients

2011 in Chiapas: Federal and State Governments Plan to Clear Community Resistance to Mega-projects

Suggested reading

Acknowledgements

About the Author

LETTERS FROM SCHOLARSHIP
RECIPIENTS: 2009

Scholarship recipients 2010
Photograph by Linda Finch

August 1, 2009
Esteemed Godmothers

Hello, I am Constancia. I live in the beautiful community of San Andrés where there are a lot of plants and trees. We plant corn, beans, peaches, apples, plums and pears. I live with my family.

I have two brothers and six older sisters and one younger sister who studies in the autonomous primary school.

I work in the kitchen with my mother. I make the tortillas. We put the vegetables and the beans on to boil. In this way we live and maintain the family.

I also want to continue studying because it is my dream ever since I finished primary school. Thank you for worrying about us with respect to our education. Many thanks for the scholarship. It inspires me more that I could have imagined. I also am going to continue ahead with weaving and handicrafts.

I say goodbye to you and hope that you are well.

Thank you, Constancia

Zinacantán, Chiapas August 2009
Hello, Dear Godmother,

I am Patricia, the scholarship recipient. I am 14 years old and I live in Zinacantán. My mother's name is Teresa and I no longer have a father because he looked for another wife. I was 9 years old when my father left.

I have two sisters and two brothers and now I study in the "telesecondary" school. I am in the second year of secondary. I hope that you help me more and I plan to continue my studies. I thank you very much for helping me with this scholarship. I don't know what to tell you more because it is the first time that I am writing you a letter.

Thank you,
Sincerely, Patricia

August 24, 2009

Hello Dear Godmothers,

I write you by means of this letter about how well I am doing in school and about the economic support that you have offered.

I want to let you know that in this past school year I have put much effort into my studies with the result that by the end of the year I was a ¨notable¨ student with a good grade point average. So I am satisfied because I achieved that grade point average. I am conscious that still I am not quite at the goal I have set for myself but I know that with effort and dedication I am going to continue to come out ahead with my studies.

Also I want to comment to you that I have been working with the women in the cooperative to familiarize myself in the different workshops with what are our rights as women.

I take advantage of this occasion to thank you infinitely for the support you have given to me because this has supported me in the expenses of my studies and I send to all of you a lot of greetings and hugs. With no more to add in this moment, I hope to be able to continue to count on your valuable support.

Sincerely, Concepción

Zinacantán

Dear Godmothers,

I hope that you all are well. I have been very well. I haven´t had problems, and these days were very good for me because I had a happy summer. But now I start classes again on August 3rd. I have practiced English a lot in school but have not as yet arrived at a decision of what I want to be when I finish. Well, in school I am studying to be an English teacher and this seems interesting to me because in the practice sessions I have had good grades.

I don't write to you very often when I am in school because I don't have much connection with the internet. When I do go to use the internet it is only to do research on some assignment that I have. But I like what I am studying. Sometimes so much homework has to be done at the same time that I feel as if I will not finish it, but I always do. Well, I am very happy because I'm in the 4th semester (*of her university career*) and still need four more. The way I am studying now is very good.

Receive many hugs and kisses and thank you for your unconditional support.

Iliana

Zinacantán, Chiapas August 1, 2009
Dear Godmothers,

I write to greet you and give you appreciation for the support you offer to us to better each day of our education. I am strengthening my knowledge. The time I have been in school I have been learning a lot.

My job working with the children is reinforcing a lot my knowledge of information technology and at the same time I learn a lot from the children also.

Coming soon in Zinacantán is the celebration of the Festival of San Lorenzo that we celebrate from August 8th to 11th. Many people celebrate and debut new clothing, as is our custom. In these days we prepare many things for the festival such as food, drinks and other things.

Well, this is what I can tell you. I hope in my next letter I can tell you more things that happen here in the town. I send you many greetings and a big hug.

Josefa

(Josefa attends university classes. Her job is due to the fact that she now has advanced computer skills. Josefa works two jobs and pays half her school fees herself.)

August 1, 2009

Dear Godmothers,

We want to thank you for the support that you offer us to continue studying. We have many desires of succeeding and finishing our primary and secondary education and what may come even further on.

As indigenous women we had no opportunity to study because our parents had no money and from earliest childhood we had to work in the fields and do domestic work.

Now we've made our own decision as women that now know their rights to continue educating ourselves and to be more independent. We want to be examples to other women who want to achieve their potential.

For now, that is all we want to say to you and many thanks for everything and for the scholarship.

Sincerely, Rosa, Eva and Marisa

P.S. We are Tojolabal women that live close to Comitán and we work in a collective that has a corn grinder and a grocery store. We have a Women´s Center where we can give legal aid to other women that need us, and we educate frequently by means of workshops.

(These are adult women who asked us for support so they could finish their primary education.)

MORE LETTERS: 2011

Chiapas, August 6, 2011

Dear Godmothers,

It gives me pleasure to inform you that I have finished preparatory school thanks to your support, and as for me I have developed educationally as much in theory as in practice. I give thanks to God for having parents that have supported me in moving ahead with my studies. Now I prepare myself to go to the university to be able to realize a huge dream of mine that would have been impossible for me because of not having the economic resources to pay for my studies. Being able to count on your continuing support I am going to study Law. Again I want to thank you infinitely for your support.

Without more to say because truly I am filled with happiness, I want to tell you with all my heart that I love you.

Please receive a cordial greeting on my part.

Respectfully, Concepción

August 6, 2011
Esteemed Godmothers,

My name is Juanita. Please receive many greetings and hugs from me and from my mamá. I want you to know that I am very happy and very enthusiastic to be able to continue my studies. Before I couldn't continue studying because of a lack of money but now that you are going to support me I will be able to continue studying. I very much want to do this, so that I can learn more and to be able to fulfill my dreams of being a textile designer.

I live in Chamula, in my community. We plant corn and beans. We have sheep, chickens and other animals. All the women get up early to make tortillas and fix the food and then afterward we tie up the sheep. I say goodbye now hoping that you are well.

Attentively, Juanita

August 1, 2011
Ocosingo, Chiapas

My name is Martina. In August I begin secondary school. I like to study to get ahead and be someone in life. I want to be the best of the students.

I am thankful to God for your having accepted me as a scholarship recipient and goddaughter.

Thanks to your support I am able to continue my studies.

Respectfully,
Martina

San Andrés de Larrainzar, Chiapas, August 5, 2011

Hello Dear Friends,

Although I don't know you very well yet, I don't doubt that you are great people and have the heart to help us.

I am very grateful to you and to God because I do believe in Him and He has put you here and given you the knowledge of your deeds. Moreover, in supporting us, I believe that your support reaches more.

I am writing this for the purpose of thanking you for your great support and I am also grateful to the organization that has permitted me to join and where I hope to stay for a long time during my life.

Judith and Linda,* I love you and wherever you may be, may God bless you and keep you always and give you a long life.

Sincerely,

Lupita

She names just the two of us because we were the ones at the bi-monthly reunion of the cooperative in August, 2011.

Crucero, San Juan Chamula, August 2011

Hello Dear Godmothers,

How have you been all this time? I hope that you find yourselves healthy and working. Because in truth it gives me much pleasure to see you again in the workshop. You are friendly and pretty and I am proud that you come again to see us.

You know that I am studying in San Cristóbal and I want to move ahead with a career in nursing. I want to help people and I know I can succeed. Thanks to you I am continuing with the career that I want so much. I am never going to be discouraged with my studies. I am just writing a few words. I just want you to be well all the time.

I appreciate your attention. Please receive a cordial greeting and many hugs.

With love, Frida

The letters thus far are my translation. This next one, however, is from Iliana, our English major. I have made no corrections.

Dear Godmothers,

I am hoping you are good.

As you know, I am almost finishing my carrer and it is an excellent thing for me because I did not disappoint you and me. I had some difficulties when I started studying my carrer but it did not break my dreams. These days, I am deciding the topic of my thesis[10] and the teacher who may help me, but it is amazing for me because I know that make a thesis is really difficult to write but I can do it. This day it is the most important thing in my life.

In the future my hope is that I may travel to the USA to get more knowledge and improve my English. Now are the important

---

[10]   A "thesis" is a paper written to complete requirements for an undergraduate degree.

things of my life but I hope you are healthy and fullness of love.

Iliana

The tears come to my eyes. Iliana will graduate from university in 2012.

2011 IN CHIAPAS: FEDERAL AND STATE GOVERNMENTS PLAN TO CLEAR COMMUNITY RESISTANCE TO MEGA-PROJECTS

Miguel Pickard - 02-marzo-2011 - San Cristóbal de Las Casas, Chiapas

The development of large infrastructure projects by Mexico's federal government and the Chiapas state government continues to advance -- rapidly where no organized opposition exists and stealthily where it does. These projects are part of the Meso-America Project (formerly known as the PPP or Plan Puebla Panama).[1] Currently the two most important mega-projects in Chiapas are (1) the Sustainable Rural Cities Project[2] (SRC) and (2) the large infrastructure projects designed to turn Chiapas into a "second Cancún" for tourism and, at the same time, an important participant in the lucrative carbon-credit trading market.

The second Sustainable Rural City in Chiapas will soon be launched in Santiago el Pinar[3] before a gala audience including President Calderón, Governor Sabines, and their respective entourages. The multi-million-dollar Sustainable Rural Cities Program could be described as a genocidal "cold war" led by Governor Sabines against the thousand-year-old rural and indigenous cultures, given its intent to clear the countryside of rural peoples, many of them indigenous, and destroy their way of life and means of production rooted in the land that many have held for centuries.

Claiming to have found "the reason behind poverty" in the "dispersion" of rural peoples in small and relatively isolated villages, the Chiapas state government has pressured rural and indigenous people to sell or turn over their land in order to relocate and concentrate them in newly built Rural Cities,. This social-engineering project was conceived mainly to benefit large corporations, which will profit from the "freed up" land. Rural families will find themselves living on tiny plots on street after street of identical houses, in a scene reminiscent of suburban sprawl in the United States. In this setting, they will be uprooted from their traditional lifestyles based on forms of production that are ecologically sound, and thrust into a capitalist economy, where they will have to meet all of their needs, including the acquisition of basic foods, through purchase in the market. They will be hostage to the meager salaries that some -- a few -- will receive in exchange for their labor in agricultural projects or in maquiladoras that are being built on land near the Rural Cities. The indigenous peoples' loss of autonomy will have begun and, over time, it will be total.

Another key project in Chiapas is the construction of a new 173 km [109 mile] toll road that will link the tourist sites of San Cristóbal de Las Casas and Palenque, current magnets for domestic and international visitors. The toll road is the backbone of a comprehensive tourism project (disguised as ecological tourism) that, in the words of Governor Sabines, will make Chiapas "the second Cancún."

Upon signing the National Tourism Agreement on February 28, 2011with entrepreneurs from the tourism industry,

Calderón committed Mexico to becoming the world's fifth largest tourism destination by 2018. According to Calderón, the agreement will "increase [Mexico's] connectivity" by land, sea and air to facilitate tourists' "arrival, travel and departure" along the main sightseeing routes. This implies "speeding up... construction of...ports and highways." Fittingly, 2011 was declared the "Year of Tourism."[(4)]

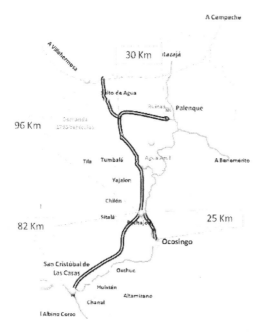

In 2009, the construction of the toll road between San Cristóbal and Palenque was stopped by mobilized groups of indigenous peoples resisting the plunder and destruction of their lands that would inevitably result from the project. Resistance by the traditional landholders and members of the Zapatista-inspired "The Other Campaign" has been centered in the communities of Mitzitón, some 15 km [10 miles] from San Cristóbal, and in San Sebastián Bachajón, municipality of Chilón, some 70 km [43.5 miles] from Palenque.

Sites of special importance to the construction of the toll road are Mitzitón, which has been designated "Kilometer Zero," or the starting point for the toll road, and San Sebastián Bachajón, which abuts the tourism sites of Agua Azul and Bolom Ajaw.

(5) In 2009, the federal government disseminated plans showing that the route of the toll road would run through traditional landholdings in Bachajón and Zapatista landholdings in Bolom Ajaw.

Given the mobilizations by organized opposition groups to the toll road, the federal and state governments, starting in 2009, decided to push forward on other fronts. Federal authorities have moved rapidly to improve the access highway to the toll road - that is, the 15 km stretch of land between San Cristóbal and Mitzitón - by adding and widening lanes and building bridges designed to handle continually increasing volumes of traffic. This work is also particularly valuable to important neighbors of the road, since the wide stretch of asphalt and sturdy overpasses will improve mobility for troops and tanks from the nearby Rancho Nuevo military base.

While the federal government levels the roadway, the state government has taken on the task of "leveling" the organized groups opposing the incursion of the road. The harassment of opposition groups in Mitzitón and Bachajón has been constant for the last several years, but conflicts have intensified in the last few weeks. In Mitzitón, this was the result of the presence of armed young evangelicals, the so-called Army of God (Ejército de Dios), the shock troops of the Eagle's Wings (Alas de Aguila) evangelical church, which reputedly has close ties to the state government. These paramilitaries have frequently attacked the majority Catholic group in Mitzitón, mostly members of The Other Campaign, who have opposed the construction of toll road on their lands, with the consequent destruction of forests, aquifers and farm land.

In Bachajón, the state government has reverted to the old tactic of wearing down the community through the arbitrary mass arrests of residents, forcing it to divert time, energy and resources into mobilizing for their release. On February 3, 2011, 117 Bachajón landholders, participants in The Other Campaign, were arrested and arraigned on charges of killing a PRI party member in a skirmish the previous day, even though only the PRI forces carried firearms. Most of the 117 were released shortly thereafter, but 10 people remain in Playas de Catazajá prison.[6] The confrontation occurred after a PRI group violently took possession of a toll booth at the entrance to the Agua Azul recreation area that was in the hands of members of The Other Campaign, because the latter had committed an intolerable act: they had begun building an ecotourism center to be run not by the government but by the local inhabitants. In the skirmish, PRI partisans destroyed the toll booth and stole building materials, including wheelbarrows, several tons of cement and assorted tools.

As one Bachajón landholder said:

> What the government is doing now is jailing those who lead the movement. As an organization we are the government's worst enemy [-] because it doesn't want us to defend what is rightfully ours [-] we know the government wants [to use] violent means to seize our ecotourism center.

People in other parts of Chiapas who have demonstrated their solidarity with the groups in Bachajón and Mitzitón have suffered similar fates of repression and detention. This was the case on February 17, when people were arrested for taking part in an act of civil disobedience by intermittently blocking the Pacific Coast highway near the town of Pijijiapan. After the blockade was lifted, the state police detained 19 people of the Coast Regional Autonomous Council (also part of The Other

Campaign). Sixteen were freed after a few hours, but lawyers from the Digna Ochoa Human Rights Center were arraigned on charges of "rioting" and inciting violence. The lawyers say that they came to the blockade merely as observers to record possible human rights violations by authorities.

In trying to discern the "logic" of state violence, analysts have noted that acts of civil disobedience seem to be a tipping point for repression. For the government, protest actions by common citizens who break laws in order to defend collective, civil and human rights are intolerable. While this remains the case, it is now evident that the state government will also resort to repression against organized groups when their protests slow down the advance of public or public/private infrastructure projects. Whether it uses a carrot or a stick, the objective is the same: to wear down and defeat opposition groups. When dialogue or negotiations fail, the government can always use the militarized police or paramilitary groups such as "God's Army" to repress opposition through incarcerations, harassment, or intimidation.

This is the "logic" or strategy behind the marked increase in recent weeks in repression against members of The Other Campaign in Chiapas. This repression is calculated to wear out groups resisting the Meso-American Project's mega-infrastructure works, not only because they oppose the neoliberal privatization and commodification of everything, but also because they propose alternative, non-capitalist forms of government, education, health, and employment. This is especially the case in the Zapatista and other communities, such as Mitzitón or Bachajón, linked to The Other Campaign, which are actually working to make these alternatives reality.

Calderón and Sabines have less than two years left in their terms to achieve significant advances in the mega-projects slated for Chiapas. The increase in repression signals the start of a campaign, in this "Year of Tourism," to clear away any opposition to making Chiapas a "green Cancún" - that is, a paradise for investors and the site of a massive resettlement experiment designed to disposses rural peoples of their land. Behind plans such as the Meso-America Project lie billions of dollars, powerful interests, and major agreements, such as the one signed recently between Chiapas and California to establish extensive "green zones" in Chiapas for the carbon credits market.[7] The people of Chiapas know little or nothing about these plans.

Translation from Spanish by the author, who gratefully thanks Carol Pryor for her editorial assistance.

Notes:

For more information on the Meso-America Project, see http://www.ciepac.org/boletines/chiapas_en.php?id=583

For more informaton on the Rural Citites Program, see http://www.ciepac.org/boletines/chiapas_en.php?id=571

The SRC of Santiago el Pinar was launched in late March 2011 after this article was originally drafted in Spanish. The first SRC is Nuevo Juan de Grijalva [translator's note].

Mexico Aims to Become World's No. 5 Tourist Destination: http://bit.ly/lXl7tA; México: Firman Acuerdo Nacional de Turismo, con la meta de estar entre los primeros cinco destinos mundiales: http://bit.ly/jwRuii

http://www.ciepac.org/boletines/chiapas_en.php?id=578

[Five people remain in prison as of this translation into English in late May 2011. (Translator's note)]

For more information on the carbon credits market in Chiapas, see http://www.ciepac.org/boletines/ chiapas_en.php?id=587

Used with permission of Miguel Pickard

SUGGESTED READINGS

Eber, Christine, and Kovic, Christine, Women of Chiapas, Routledge Publishers; New York, 2003

Gibler, John, Mexico Unconquered: Chronicles of Power and Revolt, City Lights Books, San Francisco; 2009

Greenfield, Patricia Marks, Weaving Generations Together: Evolving Creativity in the Maya of Chiapas, School of American Research, Publishers; Santa Fe, New Mexico, 2004

Kristof, Nicholas D., and WuDunn, Sheryl, Half the Sky: Turning Oppression into Opportunity for Women Worldwide, Vintage Books; 2010

Morris, Jr., Walter F., Living Maya, Harry N. Abrams, Inc., Publishers, New York; 1987

Morris, Jr., Walter F., Guía Textil de Los Altos de Chiapas (A Textile Guide to the Highlands of Chiapas), Asociación NaBolom, San Cristóbal de Las Casas; 2010

Ortiz, Teresa, Never Again a World Without Us: Voices of Mayan Women in Chiapas, Mexico, Epica Publishers; 2001

Walker, Gayle, and Suarez, Kiki, Every Woman is a World: Interviews with Women of Chiapas, University of Texas Press; 2008

ACKNOWLEDGMENTS

First and foremost, I owe a huge debt of gratitude to the women and girls in the weaving cooperative in San Cristóbal de las Casas. Without Ramona, their loyal and amazing coordinator, who became our invaluable liaison, none of this would have been possible. Thank you to Grahame Russell of Rights Action, who first connected me with Ramona and the cooperative in 2003.

In June, 2012, Carol Bell, the famous botfly woman, left the earthly plane and passed on to her greatest travel adventure. I salute her courage and am grateful for our 20-year friendship. Hugs and appreciation go to Martha Lumia, whose spirit and laughter made our 1995 travels even more wonderful. Thanks to all of you who have traveled to Chiapas with me. Thanks to the *Mujeres de Maiz OF* original board members: Linda Finch, Pat Lang, Martha Rudersdorf, Molly Rivard and Carol Bell and to the current board: Linda Finch, Molly Rivard, Martha Rudersdorf, Mary Norton, Sandy Reed, Cathy Van Ruhan and Steve Gilchrist. Cathy Van Ruhan's editing help was wonderful --- she showed admirable patience with my comma-cally challenged manuscript. Thanks to Bob who cheerfully cat-sits when I am in Chiapas and who volunteers willingly at all our events.

ABOUT THE AUTHOR

Author photo by Eric Rust

Judith Pasco taught high school Spanish for 20 years. In addition to being the Board Chair of *Mujeres de Maiz Opportunity Foundation*, she is addicted to reading, travel, and gardening. She lives in the foothills of the Olympic Mountains in Washington State with her beekeeper/carpenter husband and their four cats.

CPSIA information can be obtained at www.ICGtesting.com
Printed in the USA
BVOW081604160113

310809BV00001B/1/P